ED SUSHISE BEEF

NATTO FRIED RICE

TAK

fried

D PORK   ADOBO CHICKEN

FRIED TO

ons   SHOYU PORK   *tako poke*

SMOKED-TAKO POKE   MISO PORK   BROILED

smoked-tako poke   SARDINES AND ONIONS

raw crab poke   Kim Chee Smoked F

blackened

UBI   KALBI POTSTICKERS   RAW CRAB PO

U WATERCRESS SALAD   KORE

GARLIC LEMONGRASS PORK   *baked saln*

EBI   *garlic salt-and-pepper shrimp*

YAMPACHI   UNCLE TANA'S FRIED PRAWNS

FROM
KAU KAU
TO
Cuisine

AN ISLAND COOKBOOK, THEN AND NOW

FROM KAU KAU TO *Cuisine*

AN ISLAND COOKBOOK, THEN AND NOW

Arnold Hiura
Food Photography by Rae Huo and Dawn Sakamoto Paiva

WATERMARK
PUBLISHING

ISBN 978-1-935690-44-3

Library of Congress Control Number: 2013952302

Photo credits
6, 146, 147 (left), 181 (lower left), 196 by Eloise Hiura
10, 12 by Hawai'i State Archives
15 by Minoru Kodama
19 by John Cross
29 by Derek Paiva
176 by Arnold Hiura, Derek Kurisu and Jason Takemura
178 by Tori Toguchi
"Now" recipe photography and page 182 and 185 (lower left) by Rae Huo
"Then" recipes and all other photography by Dawn Sakamoto Paiva

SPAM is a registered trademark of Hormel Foods, LLC and is being used
with permission from Hormel Foods Corporation.

Design and production
Kurt Osaki
Stacy Fujitani
Osaki Creative Group

Watermark Publishing
1000 Bishop St., Suite 806
Honolulu, HI 96813
Telephone 1-808-587-7766
Toll-free 1-866-900-BOOK
sales@bookshawaii.net
www.bookshawaii.net

10 9 8 7 6 5 4 3 2

Printed in Korea

Contents

An Evolutionary Cookbook

Food in Hawai'i today is like a constantly shifting kaleidoscope of colorful and tasty vignettes—from elegant Hawai'i Regional Cuisine (HRC) restaurants to convenience store SPAM® musubi, from hip food trucks and pop-up restaurants to weathered old noodle shops and day-old stew and rice at grandma's house. Local food is all of these things and everything in between, and, to make sense of it, one has to embrace it all.

Although they may appear totally unrelated at first, there is often more that binds the traditional comfort foods from Hawai'i days gone by with the cutting edge cuisine of today. Welcome to *From Kau Kau to Cuisine: An Island Cookbook, Then and Now*, a fun and informative, side-by-side presentation of classic local dishes from Hawai'i's past, each paired with a contemporary dish inspired by the same flavors or ingredients. It offers, in other words, the best of both worlds.

Here, we won't delve in great detail into the history of food in Hawai'i. Providing that historical perspective was the goal of *Kau Kau: Cuisine and Culture in the Hawaiian Islands* (Watermark Publishing, 2009). Rather, we present a curated overview of where we've been, where we are and where we're headed, food-wise.

For the purposes of this book, "Then" refers simply to THEN—a romanticized, near-mythic period in Hawai'i's past that locals over the age of 50 fondly remember as "beforetime." Characterized by sugar and pineapple plantations, it was a time when people never had to lock their doors and neighbors got along with one another regardless of their racial, ethnic or cultural backgrounds—or at least that's what many people who experienced it say.

"Then" is best embodied in those aging survivors of what's been called the Greatest Generation, children of the plantation who weathered poverty, the Great Depression, World War II and more. Their memories and those of their immigrant parents and grandparents comprise the legacy passed down to their children, a now very mature generation of baby boomers.

Just as "Then" was THEN, "Now" is NOW, a time of change driven by increasingly influential members of Generations X and Y. Born into a post-plantation Hawai'i, this generation's ties to the past are limited to the old storefronts and aging plantation-era houses still standing in parts of rural O'ahu and the Neighbor Islands, black-and-white images staring back at them from time-worn family albums and stories of the past told to them by their parents and grandparents.

Fueled by the instantaneous, global impact of the Internet and social media, the food scene in the Islands today continues to evolve, led by an innovative new generation of chefs who were inspired by HRC pioneers and in whose hands the future of food in Hawai'i lies.

Experienced travelers will tell you that their most memorable journeys were the ones taken with the assistance of a great guide. *From Kau Kau to Cuisine: An Island Cookbook, Then and Now* is fortunate to feature two eminently qualified individuals for that task: the Big Island's Derek Kurisu for the Then and O'ahu's Jason Takemura for the Now. Together, they pay homage to the traditional and familiar foods rooted in our past, as well as showcase contemporary interpretations of local food through simple recipes that anyone can follow at home.

Some believe that "That was then, this is now, and never the twain shall meet." Others say, "What is old will be made new again." We invite you to embrace the connections. After all, every turn of the kaleidoscope reveals a new design—more bright and beautiful than the one before!

—Arnold Hiura

The old Pa'auilo Store building on Highway 19 on the Hilo Coast has since been torn down. Today, the store carries on in a refurbished building next door.

Part One

Kau Kau Time!
The Roots of Island Cooking

Pāpaʻikou, Hilo coast, 1963

Growing up in the Big Island plantation town of Hakalau in the 1950s and ʻ60s, Derek Kurisu experienced plantation life in its heyday. Sugar and pineapple plantations dominated the landscape of every Hawaiian island—from Kīlauea, Kauaʻi, in the north, to Nāʻālehu near the southernmost tip of Hawaiʻi Island.

At one time, in fact, the entire stretch of coastline from the Big Island's main city of Hilo out to Kohala was defined by a string of sugar plantation towns (from south to north): Wainaku, Pāʻpaikou, Pepeʻekeo, Honomū, Hakalau, Nīnole, Pāpaʻaloa, Laupāhoehoe, ʻOʻōkala, Paʻauilo, Pāʻauhau, Honokaʻa and Kohala.

Often separated by just a few miles, each town was a small world unto itself, comprised of workers' houses clustered around a mill, which was easily distinguishable by its towering smokestack. Mills were perched right along the coastline so they could jettison muddy wash water into the sea. Adjoining the mill was a garage and machine shop, which serviced and repaired the plantation's fleet of trucks and wide array of heavy equipment.

In addition, each plantation town usually included a plantation office, public school, general store, post office, barbershop, gas station, baseball field,

gymnasium, and churches of various denominations. Some of the larger towns had multiple stores, a "hospital" (dispensary), bakery and in some cases even a theater.

Mom-and-Pop Stores

Like movie sets from a bygone era, small mom-and-pop stores still dot the local landscape, from quiet country roads to busy city streets on every Hawaiian island. The "newer" ones—simple cinder block structures—are themselves mid-century relics. The original plantation-era stores are truly vintage wooden buildings, well worn with age.

In their original incarnations, plantation stores were literally "company stores," wholly owned extensions of the corporations that ran the plantations and controlled everything associated with it. Workers could acquire goods from the company store on credit using their employee identification number, or *bango*, which was stamped on a metal tag like a GI's dog tag. Payments were drawn directly from the worker's pay, often leaving the worker a negative balance come payday.

In short order, however, entrepreneurial-minded immigrants who had fulfilled the terms of their labor contracts eagerly pursued opportunities to run small neighborhood businesses. Today, faded old wooden signs usually indicate that many of these stores were run by Chinese, Japanese or Portuguese families.

These stores carried everyday staples like bread and milk, some fruits, vegetables and canned goods. "There was always a small freezer with frozen meat," Derek recalls. "Never fresh meat, always frozen."

Mainly, however, people fondly remember patronizing these stores as children entering a dream world filled with cold sodas, ice cakes, candies, pastries and ice cream. Popular snacks included: Tomoe Ame, milk candy, button candy, rock candy, dried abalone, Bazooka bubble gum, dried *ika* (squid), sour lemon and ginger chunks. Some stores specialized in shave ice or various types of "crack seed" stored in large glass jars. One's purchase was placed into a small brown paper bag that old-timers would always lick to enjoy the last bit of salty goodness off of the insides of the bags. Some stores even had wooden porches and benches out front where customers could sit and enjoy a cold soda, ice cream or shave ice, and talk story.

More workers' houses were grouped in outlying camps scattered *mauka* (upland) from the mill. There were small local dairies and chicken farms where residents could buy eggs, but lots of families kept their own chickens in backyard coops for eggs and, eventually, for the stew pot. Just a few people raised pigs, cows or goats, but almost everyone kept a garden.

Community Gardens

One of the noteworthy features of plantation life was that most camps allocated small parcels of land at no charge for workers to plant vegetable gardens. Although the physical layout of camps varied according to terrain, most plantation houses were situated rather closely together, leaving only limited space to grow things immediately alongside one's house. Land for gardens, therefore, was made available on the outskirts of the camp.

"For each family, plantation management made available a 30-by-100-foot parcel for raising vegetables," Derek's father, Yasushi "Scotch" Kurisu, wrote in his 1995 memoir, *Sugar Town: Hawai'i Plantation Days Remembered.* "Our family maintained such a plot at Wailea Mill Camp and later at Hakalau Up Camp. The mudpress from the mill's mud filter made excellent fertilizer when mixed with dried chicken manure. These ingredients were organic and free, too."

Homegrown vegetables played a major role in the daily plantation diet. Some popular crops were various types of squash, pumpkin, sweet potatoes, carrots, string beans, soybeans, *daikon* (white radish), corn, lettuce, cabbage, *won bok* (Chinese cabbage), cucumbers, eggplant, bittermelon, peanuts, taro, *yamaimo* (mountain yam) and green onions, to name a few. These were popular because of their versatility and because they grew well in Hawai'i. Some families also grew other specialty plants reflective of

The Heart of the Community

Comparing these mom-and-pop stores with modern day convenience stores would be a big mistake, Derek says. "The main difference was, instead of hired help, the old stores were owner-operated and, when you went in, you immediately knew you were dealing with the owners."

It was common practice for these stores to extend credit till payday, take orders by phone, and many even made deliveries to people's homes. "Without those small mom-and-pop stores, we wouldn't have survived," Derek says. "Because transportation was very limited, people couldn't simply go to town to buy what they needed, so they had to rely on these small country stores. These stores served as gathering places, the hub of camp life. You might say these stores were the heart of the community."

Crack seed store wares.

their ethnic background. Since crops tended to mature all at once, people routinely shared their harvests with neighbors. Pickling also allowed produce to be enjoyed beyond their limited shelf life.

These community gardens yielded more than just vegetables, however. In the dwindling sunlight after work, neighbors shared the experience of growing food and, from that common ground, grew friendships, trust and a shared sense of place.

Whereas plantation experiences elsewhere around the world tend to be remembered negatively as eras of racism, social stratification and economic exploitation, the majority of people in Hawai'i tend to celebrate the positive aspects of life on sugar and pineapple plantations. Although they did not have much in material wealth, they say, they were all the richer for the experience of lives that included a variety of ethnic and cultural backgrounds.

There was a rhythm to daily plantation life. Whistles blew. Workers gathered at the labor yard every morning in the predawn darkness. Barefoot kids walked to school. Some plantation work, including harvesting and processing, ran in three shifts, 24 hours a day. Other day laborers were home by nightfall for dinner, baths and bedtime.

What They Ate

What people ate at the time was really a reflection of everything that came before them, starting with the original Polynesian voyagers who settled these remote islands more than 1,500 years ago. They introduced taro, breadfruit, sweet potatoes, yams, sugar cane, *kukui* (candlenut) and many other edible plants, along with pigs, chickens and dogs. They fished the same ocean and foraged for food in the same mountains, forests and streams as the immigrants who followed.

Westerners left their mark, too, most notably seafarers who brought salted meat and fish (cod, salmon, butterfish) as provisions aboard their ships and introduced cattle and goats. Standard hardtack, also

Community garden, Hilo coast.

known as ship's biscuits or pilot bread, was called saloon pilot crackers in Hawai'i and remains popular today.

This era of the tall ships spawned the development of sugar and pineapple plantations, which triggered the need to import thousands of laborers from different parts of the world, including China, Portugal, Japan, Korea, Puerto Rico, the Philippines and other nations. Each ethnic group, in turn, contributed to the development of Hawai'i's local culture and cuisine.

Plantation workers from many different backgrounds brought their lunches to work in metal lunch cans called *kau kau* tins and commonly shared their lunches with each other at kau kau time (kau kau being the Hawaiian pidgin term for food). Neighbors and coworkers attended each other's weddings, funerals, baby *lū'aus* and ethnic festivals such as bon dances, further cementing the multicultural nature of plantation society.

Then came World War II, which introduced

Chicken Hekka

If a cross section of Hawai'i folks were asked to name the quintessential plantation dish, Chicken Hekka would likely top the list. In fact, when Hawai'i's Plantation Village, the outdoor historical museum on O'ahu, decided to have some fun a number of years ago, it chose to host a Chicken Hekka cook-off between teams from area high schools. It is also a sure-fire menu item when plantation towns host reunions.

Hekka is, basically, a one-pot dish with similarities to Japanese *sukiyaki*, usually made of chopped up chicken pieces (although beef or pork hekka is also popular), vegetables such as carrots, onions, green onions, celery, mushrooms and bamboo shoots, as well as long rice (cellophane or Chinese bean thread noodles). The ubiquitous plantation-food flavors of *shoyu*, sugar and ginger season the dish. (See page 42 for a recipe.)

That description is just a guideline, however, as hekka is a dish that invites individual inspirations, adjustments and embellishments. For example, some folks like adding tofu or cracking a raw egg into their hekka while still piping hot. One of the keys to hekka's popularity is that the cooking process creates a light, tasty sauce that was enough to flavor the rice that always accompanied the dish. "In the old days," one old-timer explains, "everything had to have gravy because you had to stretch everything."

Hekka fits the plantation profile perfectly, as it is not specifically Chinese, Japanese, Filipino, Portuguese or of any other ethnic origin. While it was often prepared at home, it was an immensely popular go-to dish whenever a large group of people had to be fed—a "party dish," in other words. It was frequently prepared in a large, commercial-sized wok over an outdoor fire. All of the ingredients were combined and stirred in one pot. Rice was steamed in another. Like plantation society, hekka melded ethnic influences and was enjoyed by everyone—simple, unpretentious and flavorful.

Canned Goods

They may be the perfect antithesis to everything we associate with good food today. They are not fresh, nor local. They are certainly not organic. They are, in fact, processed, swimming in sodium and packed with preservatives. Why, then, do Hawai'i folks so love and treasure canned goods?

Let us count the ways. They were affordable and would not spoil. They didn't need refrigeration or take up freezer space. Besides, even frozen food was subject to spoilage given the frequency of electrical outages in the plantation days. Canned foods not only kept well on the shelf but stood up to the heat and humidity of Hawai'i even after they were opened and prepared. This was important when workers packed their lunches in the pre-dawn darkness, then left their lunch pails outside in the sun until mealtime at midday.

Some of the most popular canned foods (and brands) were: SPAM® (Hormel), Vienna sausage (Libby's), deviled ham (Libby's), sardines (Holmes), tuna (Coral), pork and beans (Van Camp's) and corned beef (Libby's), to name a few.

Well-seasoned, canned meats encased in metal armor were tasty on their own or could be stretched and served with rice to feed many hungry mouths. They went well with eggs in an omelet, vegetables in a stir fry, or with onions. The preferred preparation was seasoned with shoyu and sugar and served with rice. Versatile, durable, packed with flavor and tasty with bread, rice, *poi* or potatoes—what's not to love about food in a can?

SPAM® to the local diet, along with a wide variety of canned goods. The spirit of Americanization ruled the postwar period, along with the popularity of hot dogs, hamburgers and drive-in restaurants.

The Art of Foraging

People were extremely resourceful when it came to obtaining food for their families. Some fished and gathered edibles from the ocean, such as varieties of seaweed (*limu* in Hawaiian, *ogo* in Japanese), sea urchin (*wana, uni*), sea cucumber (*namako*) and limpets (*'opihi*). In the real old days, people ate turtle, too.

Others headed mauka to hunt wild pigs and pick bamboo shoots, watercress and fern shoots such as fiddlehead (*hō'i'o* in Hawaiian, *warabi* in Japanese) and *kakuma* (tree fern, *hāpu'u* in Hawaiian). The rivers yielded shrimp (*'ōpae*), frogs, and goby fish (*o'opu* in Hawaiian, *gori* in Japanese).

Kids roamed the countryside searching out all sorts of fruits, such as lychee, mangoes, vi apples, mountain apples, rosy apples, oranges, tangerines, *waiawī* (cherry guava), longan, soursop, starfruit, breadfruit, papaya, bananas, peach, persimmon, even plums in cooler climates, pineapples, *pohā* berries, *liliko'i, poka, 'ōhelo* berries and *pānini* (cactus fruit), to name a few. (See pages 128 and 146 for more on Island-style foraging.)

Soup Kitchens

Not all childhood memories are pleasant ones, of course. And for kids growing up on a plantation, there was nothing more humbling than having to endure the indignities of a long, protracted labor strike—especially having to rely on union-sponsored soup kitchens for their meals.

When paychecks were not forthcoming, soup kitchens were set up in camp clubhouses, social halls and churches to feed striking workers and their families. They were organized and run by volunteer committees that would ideally include one or two individuals with some prior institutional experience cooking at schools or possibly in the military. After all, some of these soup kitchens had to feed up to several hundred people every day.

Food was obtained through a variety of means. Individuals grew vegetables in their home gardens and donated them to the soup kitchens. Some groups cleared and planted large-scale strike gardens. Hunting and fishing parties were organized, while so-called "bumming committees" solicited donations from businesses and other supporters. Family relatives who lived outside the plantations and pensioners also chipped in to help. Supply committees purchased meat, pork and fish at greatly reduced prices from sympathetic storeowners and farmers. The strike committees did their best to put out the best meals they could with what they had. The menu often included hekka (chicken, beef or pork) and rice, lots of vegetables, and, yes, cauldrons of soup.

Most soup kitchens were eat-in operations, where individuals brought their own plates and utensils, stood in line to be served, and then sat and ate along with others. In some places, a family representative could bring a pot or bowl to take food home to eat. In yet another scenario, food items such as rice, canned milk, vegetables and fish were distributed directly to families in proportion to the size of each family unit.

Shipping Strikes

Isolated in the middle of the Pacific, Hawai'i's people view shipping strikes with great trepidation. It's no wonder, since the state depends on cargo ships to deliver an estimated 80 percent or more of its goods. Hawai'i imports some $10 billion worth of products each year; a little more than $1 billion of that is food. It was once estimated that about 65 percent of Hawai'i's annual food consumption arrived from outside the Islands; today that estimate approaches 85 or 90 percent.

One might argue that the fear of shipping strikes is ingrained in the DNA of Islanders, even if in reality only a few major strikes have significantly impacted the state's economy. One of these occurred in 1949, when the ILWU (International Longshore and Warehouse Union) staged a strike that shut down all shipments to and from Hawai'i for 177 days. Another major shipping strike was the 100-day West Coast dockworkers' strike of 1971. Many Hawai'i residents recall the shortages of food and other goods caused by that walkout, which is the main reason why people stockpile certain durable goods year-round and can fly into a panic at any suggestion of a shipping strike.

In 1999, for example, talk of a possible strike prompted shoppers to rush to local stores in search of food, paper goods and other items deemed essential to survival in the Islands. In 2002, a lockout of dockworkers at West Coast ports stirred up nervousness among local businesses and residents facing a slowdown in the shipment of goods between Hawai'i and the West Coast.

As a youngster, Derek looked forward to shopping trips in Hilo with his family. Although the trip to town was less than 30 minutes away, it was a real adventure for country kids. As with almost everyone else, the trip always came on or right after payday, and the family's shopping list was aimed to cover its major needs for the month. Topping the list were staples like a 100-pound bag of rice and a gallon of shoyu (soy sauce) from Taniguchi Store (now KTA).

Between shopping expeditions to town, everyday items such as bread and milk were purchased from the local store. Charges were billed once a month. Those living in outlying camps could also look forward to regular visits from the fish peddler and vegetable man (who also sold fresh tofu) who would arrive in trucks filled with perishables on ice.

ILWU picket line, Hakalau.

The Decline of Sugar and Pine

Lives were so completely dictated by this close lifestyle that it was almost inconceivable to think the plantations would ever close. Back in the 1930s, Hawai'i's sugar plantations employed more than 50,000 workers and produced more than one million tons of sugar a year. In 1959, the year Hawai'i was granted statehood, about 221,000 acres of land on four islands were devoted to raising sugar cane. At the time sugar brought in about $150 million each year, with a payroll of some $56 million. From the 1960s through the mid-'80s, Hawai'i continued to produce about a million tons of sugar a year.

But then came the fall, caused primarily by sugar produced more economically overseas—in Brazil, India, China, Thailand, Pakistan, Mexico, Colombia, Australia, Argentina, the Philippines and elsewhere. In the decade from 1985 to 1995, the number of people employed in the sugar industry plummeted from 9,000 to about 2,000. The number of sugar companies shrank from 12 to five. Sugar production shrank by more than half from one million to 492,000 tons in 1995.

Today, the Hawaiian Commercial and Sugar Company on Maui operates the only mill still producing Hawaiian cane sugar. It employs nearly 800 people and produces approximately 200,000 tons of cane sugar a year.

Pineapple was second only to sugar cane in Hawai'i's economic hierarchy. In 1923, Dole was the largest pineapple packer in the world. Between 1930 and 1940, Hawai'i dominated the global canned pineapple industry and was considered the pine capital of the world, growing about 85 percent of the world's pineapple. In the 1950s, there were eight companies operating in Hawai'i. At its peak, pineapple employed close to 4,000 people and produced $107 million worth of crops.

Hawai'i's pineapple industry began to decline in the 1960s. Its share of the world's production dropped from 72 percent in the 1950s to just 33 percent by 1973. The record for pineapple production in Hawai'i was set in 1955 at 1.5 million tons. In 2006, the state produced just 188,000 tons of fresh pineapple. Today, fewer than 1,200 workers are employed by the pineapple industry in Hawai'i.

Bug Juice Then & Now

Country kids loved to dip or soak tart, unripe fruits like green guava, green mango or vi apple in a sauce they commonly called "bug juice." Derek recalls that the primary ingredients in bug juice were shoyu, sugar and vinegar, although almost everyone had their own secret ingredients that, of course, made their sauce infinitely better than everyone else's. By packing a small container of their prized bug juice in their schoolbags, kids could pick fruits after school and quickly concoct a satisfying snack for free.

They surely weren't aware of it at the time, but the practice of eating fruit with salt or shoyu is widespread throughout Asia and other parts of the world. Besides green mango and guava, salt is commonly used to lightly season fruits like honeydew melon, watermelon, pears and papaya. Some say that the salt enhances the sweetness of ripe fruit and reduces the bitterness of green fruit.

Other variations on the theme include blending *li hing* powder and salt, cayenne pepper and salt, *bagoong* (fish sauce) and pepper, and substituting lime juice in place of vinegar. Thai green papaya salad, for example, is seasoned with a dressing that includes fish sauce, sugar, salt and lime juice, and honeydew melon is popularly paired with the savory saltiness of prosciutto ham.

The tradition of keeping a container of sauce close at hand also carried over as those country kids grew older, Derek says. "We kept a bottle of chili pepper water and shoyu—or shoyu, vinegar, sugar and chili pepper—in the trunks of our car. This came in handy when we went fishing or diving and caught certain types of reef fish, like *palani*, and we would *pūlehu* (grill) the fish whole—guts and all. Peel off the skin, dip the meat in the sauce—it was great with cold beer. Some say even better than lobster!"

For thousands of Hawai'i residents, working in pineapple canneries and fields was much more than a paycheck; it was a rite of passage. As teenagers, a generation of baby boomers went to work at the canneries and fields during summer vacation to earn spending money, help ease the strain on family budgets and pay for college. Just about any able-bodied applicant was hired. Jobs were full time (40 hours a week) temporary at minimum wage, which in the mid-1960s was $1.25 an hour.

Today many veterans of summer cannery work say the experience was their first "real" job, one that taught them the value of a dollar. It also served as a great democratizing force, since it was one of the few places where kids who lived

Get Rice?

Perhaps what is most telling about strike scenarios—besides underscoring the growing importance of sustainability, food independence and supporting local food producers—is what they say about what Islanders value most when it comes to survival and well-being. The first item to disappear off supermarket shelves is rice, Derek says, followed by canned goods such as SPAM® and Vienna sausage, paper goods such as toilet tissue and paper towels, cases of bottled water and bags of dry dog food.

At the first hint of a run on goods, supermarkets are quick to post signs placing limits on specific products—especially rice. Derek remembers that as the 1971 strike dragged on, KTA SuperStores' management broke open their remaining 100-pound bags of rice and repacked them into five-pound bags. These were given to those who needed it the most, he said, like families with young children, the sick and the elderly. "Rice is so precious; there is no substitute for rice in Hawai'i—not bread or potatoes. People in Hawai'i need their rice."

Sharing the Same Boat

"We didn't want to go soup kitchen," Derek recalls, "but our parents made us go." Even worse, he said, was having to stand in a special line in school in order to get lunches when there was a strike on. "We felt like the others were looking at us."

At the time Derek's family was living in an area of Hakalau called Wailea. "The soup kitchen was set up at a church located where Akiko's Buddhist Bed and Breakfast is now," Derek adds. "We used to bring our own plates, wait in line to be served and sit down to eat right there."

There's a lot about those soup kitchens that the people who experienced them would just as soon forget. But there were also lasting lessons learned. Everyone had to pull together to get through the hard times. Everyone ate together. Everyone was in the same boat.

in different areas and attended different schools mingled and worked side by side. Even Hawai'i's gaping private-public school chasm could be bridged when students labored together at the cannery.

Overall, pineapple and sugar workers lived similarly hard plantation lifestyles. The workday usually started at 6:00 in the morning and ended anywhere between 2:00 and 4:30 in the afternoon, depending on a person's role in the mills or fields.

In spite of the hard work and low pay, many look back at the plantation era in Hawai'i with a strong sense of nostalgia and sentimentality. The hot sun, sharp leaves and noisy machinery are memories that pale beside the recollection of the social cohesion and sense of security that permeated the plantation lifestyle. It's no wonder that the closure of the plantations had such a significant impact on the lives and psyches of Hawai'i's people.

Teaching Every Man to Cook

On an almost daily basis, shoppers at KTA will find Derek at the front entrance or walking through the aisles greeting customers—most of them by name. "I get really sad when I see a customer who's lost his wife," he says. "A lot of these older guys never learned to cook, so they're lost without their wives. They come into the store and they don't know the first thing about feeding themselves. They can't even boil a package of instant noodles, so many of them end up eating out all the time.

"I want to help them. My mission is to teach every single man to cook. I try to get them over their fear of trying—show them how to shop, how to use the stove, handle pots and pans. I show them how easy it is to cook for themselves, how to use the microwave oven. I tell them that the easiest thing to make is pūpū because when you're drinking, everything tastes so 'ono!"

Derek's aunt and grandmother's former sewing shop, Hakalau, 2013

Food Brings People Together

These days, Derek spends much time out in the community, cooking up quick, simple and delicious local-style meals at group events, schools and senior citizen centers. He uses every opportunity to reach out, teach and promote an appreciation of the spirit of aloha.

He reaches out to young people in particular, encouraging them to take the time to learn dishes that are special to their families. "When your family has a potluck," he tells them, "you should learn how to make your aunty's famous salad or your uncle's 'ono chicken, because they're part of your family tradition. Once they're gone, it's going to be too late. Find out what pots and pans they use and make sure you keep them, because you're going to need that. That's the ones that somehow hold the magic. The whole spirit stay in them."

Much of Derek's outreach work centers on the enjoyment to be found in preparing meals and in the communal aspects of food. "I try to make cooking fun, make it cool to cook," he says. "I try to make the young kids and old guys laugh." Derek's bottom line? "To me, food is entertainment. It's fun. If you have fun when you cook, the food tastes better. Every day I get home from work and start cooking, maybe with a beer or glass of wine. It feels good to be home. I forget about the stresses of work, relax and enjoy life. Food is a tool that brings people together. Even in the old days, plantation workers shared their lunches with each other. Today, we get together with friends and family and have potluck."

Derek Kurisu's dedication to featuring old-style ingredients and championing the simple meals that people enjoyed together feeds more than bellies. For in them we also find all the savory flavors—and the many shared values—that make Hawai'i so special.

A Timeline of Plantation Closures

1969   Waimea Sugar Company on Kaua'i closes.

1970   'Ewa Plantation merges with O'ahu Sugar Company (Waipahu).

1971   Sugar operations in Wainaku, Hakalau, Pepe'ekeo and Pāpa'ikou are consolidated into Hilo Coast Processing Cooperative. Two years later, Pepe'ekeo Sugar merges with Mauna Kea Sugar to form Mauna Kea Sugar Company.

1971   Kahuku Sugar Mill closes on O'ahu.

1972   Hutchinson Sugar Plantation Co. combines with Hawaiian Agricultural Company to create Ka'ū Sugar Company.

1972   Pā'auhau Sugar's assets are purchased by Honoka'a Sugar Company.

1972   Libby sells its Moloka'i pineapple operations to Dole.

1973   Kohala Sugar Company closes.

1976   Dole closes its Maunaloa pineapple plantation (originally Libby, McNeill & Libby) on Moloka'i.

1978   Honoka'a Sugar Company merges with Laupāhoehoe Sugar Company. Francis S. Morgan purchases the entity in 1984 and renames it Hāmākua Sugar Company.

1982   'Ola'a Sugar Company closes.

1991   Dole closes its Honolulu cannery.

1992   Dole closes its pineapple plantation on Lāna'i. In 1922, James Dole had purchased the entire island of Lāna'i and turned it into the world's largest pineapple plantation, with 20,000 acres and more than 1,000 workers and their families.

1994   Pepe'ekeo Sugar Company (also known as Hilo Coast Processing Company) closes.

1993   Hāmākua Sugar Company closes. Over 400 families were left without work. Ten years earlier, it had employed more than twice that number.

1995   O'ahu Sugar Company, the leading sugar producer on O'ahu, ceases operations.

1996   Ka'ū Sugar Company closes.

1996   Waialua Sugar Company, the last sugar plantation on O'ahu, closes. At its height, the company had employed nearly 2,000 workers.

1999   Pioneer Mill in Lāhainā, Maui closes.

2000   Līhu'e and Kekaha sugar mills merge before closing in November 2000.

2008   Del Monte ceases all operations after 90 years in Hawai'i. The closure leaves about 700 pineapple workers without jobs.

2009   Maui Land & Pineapple shuts down all pineapple operations after a century of operating on Maui.

2010   On Kaua'i, Gay & Robinson harvests its final sugar cane crop.

VIA Gelato, one of the many roaming food trucks using social media to communicate with customers.

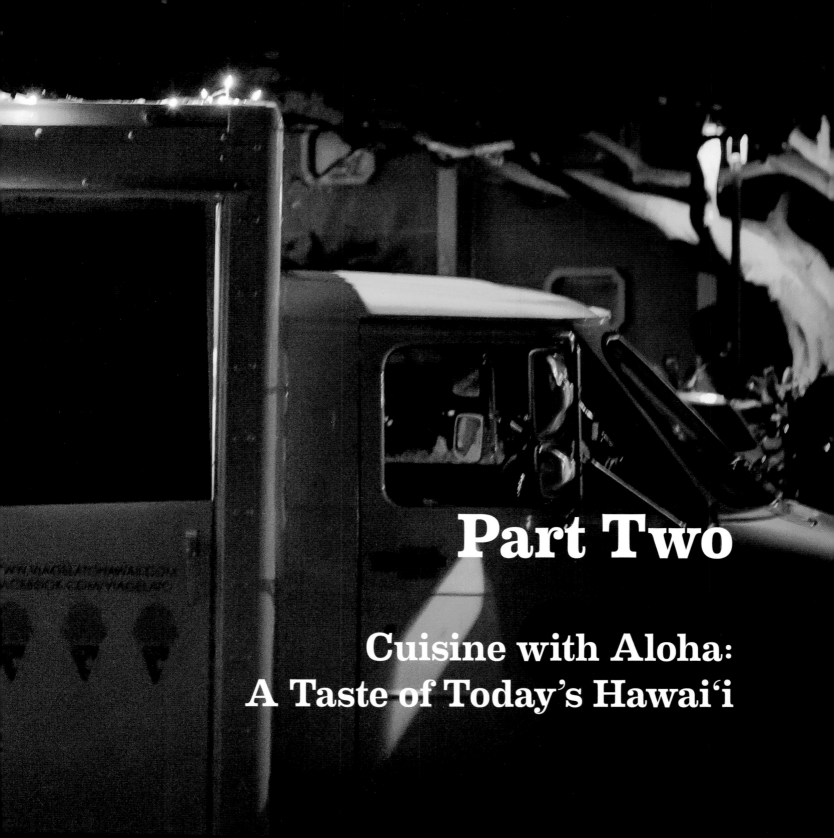

Part Two

Cuisine with Aloha:
A Taste of Today's Hawai'i

Old school or new school?

Returning to Hawai'i in 2003 was quite a culture shock for Jason. After all, it's no secret that the Islands often lag behind the Mainland when it comes to the latest fads. Local folks of the appropriate vintage (60-ish) can remember when snowy black-and-white television shows were broadcast in Hawai'i a week or two after the rest of the country had seen them. Even all of the sporting events were aired on a delayed basis. (Imagine watching games already knowing who won!) The same held true when it came to the latest trends in music, fashion and food, which could take weeks, months—or even years—to finally wash up on these shores.

"I felt that Hawai'i was so way behind the times," Jason says of his homecoming 10 years ago. "But a lot has changed since then," he says, referring to both his personal approach to food as well as changes in Hawai'i's dining public.

Regardless of its reaction time to Mainland trends, this much is certain: Food in Hawai'i continues to branch out and grow at its own exponential pace. "Locals travel a lot more—both to the Mainland and foreign countries," Jason observes. "They are more knowledgeable than in the past, more adventuresome and their expectations are higher." Television, the Internet, smart phones and social media also help to keep Hawai'i on a closer pace with the rest of the country. And, as sometimes happens, Mainland trends have circled around so far that our own "old" traditions are now part of *au courant* "new" movements on the continent—food trucks and mixed-plate, home-style ethnic cuisine, anyone?

So much has changed that many visitors to the Islands who were once routinely herded through forgettable "Hawaiian"-themed hotel buffets now plan their trips specifically around food-related and agri-tourism activities. Top Island chefs, restaurants and culinary schools have earned recognition overseas and talented young chefs from the Islands have found success in national

Fresh out of culinary school in Oregon, Chef Jason Takemura spent several years soaking up the vibe of the Monterey-Carmel-Pebble Beach region—one of the hotbeds of California's culinary scene. Known as "California's Salad Bowl," the area is home to dozens of hip, exclusive restaurants, farmers markets, vineyards and roadside stands of all shapes, sizes and specialties—so many, in fact, that it's said you can visit a farmers market any day of the week there.

A favorite activity of Jason and his chef compatriots was something they called "Black Box parties," a variation on the classic *Iron Chef* contests. One or more participants would shop for local specialty foods and other interesting ingredients that they would then place in a black box. A designated chef would receive the box and use the mystery ingredients to prepare a meal for the others. It was just the sort of fun and creative challenge that a young chef thrived on.

cooking competitions. Elegantly produced food festivals and dozens of high-profile fundraising events featuring Hawai'i's top chefs crowd the social calendars of many well-heeled local residents. What are some of the hottest trends in the world of local cuisine?

Hawai'i Food Trends—Streetwise and Casual

Many of Hawai'i's most-talked-about food trends in recent years actually relate to how the food is delivered, rather than the food itself. Take, for example, the popularity of food trucks and pop-up restaurants led by rising Gen-X chefs, with support from a correspondingly younger customer base.

While lunch wagons and drive-ins have long been a part of the local kau kau landscape, food trucks today more closely emulate the ones that started in California in the early 2000s. Traditional lunch wagons remain popular—especially around beaches, industrial areas, construction sites, downtown office buildings and college campuses—because they consistently serve up tasty and filling local plate lunches at affordable prices. The new-generation food trucks tend to focus on a few specialty items and rely mainly on food festivals, special events and social media to reach their prime audiences.

Once a month, the Kaka'ako area of Honolulu plays host to the Eat the Street food truck and street food rally. Launched in January 2011, the event continues to grow, with anywhere from a dozen to more than 40 food trucks and street food vendors gathering on any given occasion. Eat the Street is free to the public and draws crowds ranging from several hundred to several thousand participants. Organizers like to change up the theme of each event and the mobility of these food trucks allows them to stage similar events in other parts of O'ahu, such as Kailua and Mililani.

Also following close on the heels of food trucks and street fairs is the growing popularity of pop-up restaurants, which make use of existing—generally underutilized—kitchen and restaurant facilities.

"Pop-ups" are proving popular with younger chefs because they are temporary, require relatively low overhead expenses and offer access to full kitchens and prep space that food trucks lack. Young chefs on the rise can maximize the opportunities offered by pop-ups to feature their specialty dishes, gain some name recognition and start building a loyal fan base before taking the plunge into the business of restaurant ownership and operation.

For local chefs, the desire to offer good-quality local food in informal settings has picked up steam in recent years. In 2005, for example, Chef Elmer Guzman—whose curriculum vitae in a nutshell includes Kapi'olani Community College (KCC), Alan Wong's, the Greenbrier, Emeril Lagasse and Sam Choy—opened the takeout-style Poke Stop in Waipahu. Brothers Gregg and Glenn Uyeda (Le Cordon Bleu-Le Bernardin) followed with The Alley restaurant at 'Aiea Bowl, and Mark "Gooch" Noguchi (KCC-Culinary Institute of America-Kona Village Resort-Town-Chef Mavro), made a big splash at the modest He'eia Kea General Store & Deli on a pier in Windward O'ahu. Gooch then moved on to establish

Events like the Hawai'i Food and Wine Festival showcase local, national and international chefs.

'Nalo Greens

One of the first—and still one of the most prominent—locally sourced HRC products is 'Nalo Greens, the specialty of 'Nalo Farms in Waimānalo, O'ahu. Developed in 1988 through a collaboration between 'Nalo Farms owner Dean Okimoto and chef Roy Yamaguchi, 'Nalo Greens is a blend of various types of tender, leafy greens that are planted, harvested and served together. The composition of the mixes can be varied to achieve different results—from spicy to slightly bitter blends, or to achieve certain colors or textures. Today, 'Nalo Farms supplies approximately 120 restaurants with more than 3,000 pounds of its specialty greens every week.

Known elsewhere as mesclun greens, 'Nalo Greens have become so popular in Hawai'i that the name is often used generically to describe similar products even if they were grown on other local farms.

One of the first changes Jason made after assuming the role of executive chef at the Pagoda was to replace the restaurant's generic tossed salad mix, which came bagged from the Mainland, with locally grown 'Nalo Greens. Jason recalls that swapping out the greens was more complicated than he had imagined. At first, some customers balked at the change, asking, "How come your salad costs more now?" The difference in quality, he explained to them, was well worth the difference in price. To drive his point home, Jason staged a blind taste test with his wait staff, serving the 'Nalo Greens and the old salad greens side by side. The outcome was 100 percent in favor of 'Nalo Greens. "After that, it got a little easier," Jason says, "and it was easier for the staff to explain the changes to our regular customers. The price is a little more than the old price, but still very reasonable."

Taste Table, a Kakaʻako venue featuring pop-ups five days a week with a rotating schedule of chefs and half the dining space located in an open alley out back. Dozens of other Gen-X chefs have likewise chosen to forego traditional fine dining or resort venues to flash their skills at small corner delis, burger stands, noodle shops and bars, where the trend towards small plates also continues to flourish.

Small plate, or "share plate," dining is proving popular because it allows customers to sample a wider range of dishes, discourages overeating induced by oversized entrees and offers more economical options in the face of ever-escalating food costs. "Gastropubs," which had their start in England, and "tapas," which are Spanish in origin, have caught on in the United States. In Hawaiʻi, local pūpū bars and Japanese *izakaya* and sushi bars have long celebrated the joys of small plate dining, especially when accompanied with beer, wine, *sake* or beverage of choice.

Hawaiʻi Regional Cuisine

The many Island culinary trends still do not directly address the question: What goes onto local plates these days? To really understand what's happening in Hawaiʻi food today, Jason says, we must start with the impact made by the pioneering chefs who founded Hawaiʻi Regional Cuisine (HRC). The seeds of HRC cuisine were sown in the 1980s and formalized at a momentous gathering of 12 influential chefs in 1991. The majority of today's Gen-X chefs who are now developing their own style and carving out their own reputations were inspired by and trained under that first generation of HRC chefs.

First and foremost, HRC promoted the use of fresh, local ingredients to create innovative dishes inspired by the flavors of Hawaiʻi's diverse ethnic cultures. It honors the skill and labor of local farmers, ranchers, fishermen and food producers, and pays homage to the food that local people grew up eating. HRC chefs apply their skill and training to reinterpret these classic dishes to meet the highest culinary standards.

A review of contemporary food trends—as identified by various Hawaiʻi media food writers and bloggers—further underscores the fact that the fundamentals of HRC remain the driving force behind Hawaiʻi's ongoing culinary evolution. With several notable tweaks, its emphasis on local food, ingredients and flavors remains the core principle guiding the current food scene.

"Locavore" and "farm-to-table" are just two of the popular terms used to describe the recently chic movement to promote the use of locally grown food that is spreading across the U.S. They also define the philosophy at the heart of HRC.

Farmers Markets

The immense popularity of farmers markets in Hawaiʻi is also rooted in the HRC movement. The farmers market in downtown Hilo traces its roots back to 1988, when a small handful of growers began selling their goods from parked cars and trucks. The Hilo Farmers Market has now grown to more than 100 vendors selling fresh fruits and vegetables, flowers, prepared food products and craft items.

An unabashed celebration of locally produced food, farmers markets have swept across the Hawaiian Islands like a great wave. Today, Hawaiʻi's largest and most popular market takes place every Saturday at Kapiʻolani Community College on the slopes of Diamond Head. The KCC Farmers Market was founded by Dean Okimoto and food writer Joan Namkoong in 2003 on behalf of the Hawaiʻi Farm Bureau Federation (HFBF). As at the other HFBF markets on Oʻahu and the Big Island, the fresh food sold at the market must be Hawaiʻi-grown; prepared foods must utilize Hawaiʻi-grown products as well.

With more than 60 vendors offering everything from produce to prepared food, several travel writers have ranked the KCC Farmers Market as one of the 10 best farmers markets in the country. The estimated 8,000 to 10,000 people who regularly jam the market between its 7:30 a.m. opening and 11 a.m. closing would seem to agree. A significant percentage of these patrons are tourists, led by a large contingent of visitors from Japan looking for an authentic Hawai'i experience. The KCC Farmers Market is known for much more than its impressive selection of fresh fruits, vegetables, flowers, Island-raised grass-fed beef and locally farmed seafood. Many people go simply to eat, partaking of the wide variety of ready-to-eat snacks, plate lunches, desserts, baked goods, handmade pastas, jams and jellies, gourmet coffee and smoothies.

The success of the KCC Farmers Market has, in turn, spawned dozens more like it throughout the state—so much so, in fact, that one would be hard pressed to find an area of Hawai'i without some form of farmers market within a reasonable distance. Some are open on weekends, others on selected weekdays. There are even evening markets.

Grass-Fed Beef

Another local agricultural success story well over 10 years in the making is the development of grass-fed beef in Hawai'i. As it was across the rest of the country, the cattle industry began as an entirely grass-fed operation, since grain was scarce and very expensive. With the development of feedlots, however, grain-finished beef rose to prominence and grass-fed meat was relegated to an inferior status, leaner and "grassier" in taste than customers' preferences demanded.

After Hawai'i's major feedlot and slaughterhouse operation on O'ahu closed in 1991, local ranchers began shipping their calves to the Mainland and Canada to be finished and taken to market. Ten years ago, about three-fourths of all cattle sold in Hawai'i were for export.

The grass-fed beef initiative led by local agricultural specialists started gaining momentum around 1995. This was a complex process that

Many restaurants and hotels have added their own chefs' gardens on-site.

involved evaluating various breeds of cattle, developing low-stress animal handling techniques, growing ideal forage grasses and working with meat processors to refine processing and tenderizing techniques in order to achieve high-quality beef.

Today, producing grass-fed beef requires that ranchers follow strict practices and procedures. After a pasture is rested, the new tips of growing grass contain the most protein. Cattle are moved through the pastures in a defined rotation to utilize the forage most efficiently. These forage-finished cattle are raised entirely on grass, all natural and free from hormones and antibiotics. Grass-fed beef has been proven to be leaner and lower in calories. It is rich in "healthy" fats and low in fats linked to diabetes, obesity and cardiovascular disease.

Back to the Future?

Compared to many other culinary hotspots across the country, Hawai'i tends to maintain a stronger connection to its traditional and ethnic local dishes. If anything, many experts believe that tradition will play an even bigger role in Hawai'i's culinary future. Consumers, they predict, will seek out heritage foods that Native Hawaiians ate, for example, delve deeper into the traditional foods from ethnic cultures that have made Hawai'i home, and gravitate to dishes that have evolved from Hawai'i's fishing, ranching,

Foraging at Farmers Markets

Jason and his family are regulars at the KCC Farmers Market held every Saturday. So much so, in fact, that Jason says, "We know our way around the vendors like the backs of our hands." In Jason's case, many of the vendors are his friends, but anyone can talk directly to the farmers and food producers and learn about their products—how they are grown and how to best prepare them. "Customers can eyeball what the vendors have and then get some advice," he says.

"We don't eat too much at the restaurant vendors at the market," Jason notes. "We go primarily to stock up our fridge at home. It's all local, and there's a huge difference in farmers market quality!"

Farmers markets bring the work of foraging home, for modern-day folk who can't or don't want to venture into the forests and streams. A walk through the market will yield unusual fruits and items like warabi or mountain apples that aren't farmed large-scale. You might even find a "guy who knows a guy" that can procure 'ōpae or 'opihi.

farming and plantation experiences. The push to eat local will remain as strong as ever and is even likely to grow with a few new twists along the way.

- **Hyper-local sourcing.** This applies to restaurants that actually maintain their own gardens, including those with planter boxes out back. It would make sense that home gardens be considered "hyper-local," too.
- **Foraging.** It's becoming cool again to gather and prepare foods that grow naturally where one lives. This includes harvesting edible plants such as berries, nuts and mushrooms from the wild. Foraging was widely practiced in Hawai'i's past, including wild fern shoots like warabi and kakuma, bamboo shoots, coconuts, breadfruit, watercress and various fruits.
- **Artisanal products.** When applied to food, "artisanal" refers to foods that are not mass-produced through mechanized methods. Rather, these tend to be handmade food products based on processes and techniques that have been handed down through generations and are possibly in danger of being lost.
- **Recipe revival.** Fueled by locavores, foragers, artisans and food historians, "recipe revival" refers to the effort to retrieve recipes from the past and put them to use in modern kitchens.
- **Snout (or Nose)-to-Tail, or Tongue-to-Tail.** Call it what you will, chefs, ranchers and hunters have butchered whole animals for all of human history. This trend, therefore, hearkens back to the very roots of cooking. Restaurants are increasingly buying whole animals from their procurers—and often direct from the ranchers or farmers who raise the animals—and breaking them down in-house, rather than ordering package upon package of the most popular cuts. The whole-animal trend goes hand-in-hand with the skyrocketing popularity of charcuterie, which refers to salting, smoking and curing prepared meat products—usually pork—such

Tako (octopus) time.

as bacon, ham, sausages and patés. These techniques of preparing meat were originally intended to help preserve meat but are now practiced primarily to achieve flavor. Food writers predict that both snout-to-tail and charcuterie practices will continue to grow in popularity, featuring new cuts of meat and putting all parts of the animal to use.
- **Blood.** A good example of extreme snout-to-tail preparation is the use of blood in such dishes as blood pancakes and sauces thickened with blood. Locals have long enjoyed dishes such as blood sausages and *dinuguang* (Filipino blood pudding stew).
- **Fermentation.** Fermentation is one of the oldest forms of food preservation—one that yields strong, distinctive flavors. Yogurt, beer, wine and cheese are just some examples of fermented foods. People in Hawai'i are very familiar with fermented items such as *kim chee*, *kombucha* (tea), *natto* (soybeans) and *bagoong*, to name a few. Like fermentation, smoking

You Eat What?

Oxtail soup—and Jason's modern Kim Chee Oxtail Fried Rice—are the sort of dishes that demonstrate that although Hawai'i may not be quick to adopt some contemporary food trends, it may be a step or two ahead of the curve when it comes to others. "What's unique about Hawai'i is the ingredients and the way we combine those ingredients," Jason explains. "When it comes to food, we truly are a melting pot. No one on the Mainland is exposed to the cultural mix that we have here. Over time, we've developed our own classic local style. Besides oxtail, take a dish like Adobo Fried Rice. In parts of the Mainland, people don't even know what *adobo* is. It's the sort of classic blending of cultures that separates Hawai'i from the rest of the country."

On this tiny island chain, Hawai'i people take for granted their exposure to far-flung cuisines and the ingredients—spices, cuts of meat, fruits, vegetables and other plant parts—that various ethnic groups have eaten for generations. In other words, Islanders know about more than just steak and potatoes.

Big Island charcuterie selection.

and drying food are not only ancient means of preservation, but also add distinctive flavors to food. The popularity of Southern barbecue attests to this, while people in Hawai'i focus on beef jerky, smoked pork and dried and smoked fish.

Buy Fresh, Buy Local

This Hawai'i agriculture slogan makes sense when you think about the long distances that imported food travels to get to the Islands. Chefs insist that fresher food means better-tasting food. Not only that, but fresh food lasts longer in the kitchen—a head of lettuce, container of mushrooms or carton of milk bought locally will last days, or even weeks, longer than its Mainland-sourced counterpart, giving home cooks more opportunities to use up all of an item before it spoils.

Almost immediately after taking the helm at the Pagoda, Jason began converting the restaurant's menu to locally sourced ingredients. "When I got here, the majority of the food on the buffet was either frozen or canned, including frozen veggies and frozen fish," he reports. Because he already had an established network of local vendors via his years at the Hukilau, it was not hard for Jason to feature more and more fresh local products throughout his Pagoda menu wherever possible.

Aside from locally grown produce, one of the most popular products Jason added to the Pagoda's revamped buffet menu is fresh Hawaiian kampachi, which has been farmed in the deep seas off the Kona Coast of the Island of Hawai'i since 2001. Kona kampachi is part of Hawai'i's growing aquaculture industry, which has doubled in value in a decade or so—to $30 million in 2010. Moi, tilapia, shrimp, seaweed, lobster, abalone, catfish, prawns and flounder are some of the other seafood products being raised. It is a significant development that at least begins to address concerns over overfishing of Hawaiian waters and recalls the important role that

The Buta Kau Kau Man

One of the most memorable symbols of this no-waste principle was the buta kau kau man. ("*Buta*" is the Japanese word for pig.) In the not-too-distant past, nearly every household in Hawai'i kept a small pail or coffee can near the kitchen sink. In the days before garbage disposals, nearly all food waste—from vegetable peelings to whatever could be scraped off of one's dinner plate—went into the can. The contents of the can were then transferred to a larger bucket located outside the home. These were usually five-gallon cans—some round, some square—with lids. They were kept near the kitchen door or hung up off the ground in the backyard. Then, on a regular basis, a local pig farmer would come and empty the scraps into cans slung over his shoulder and transfer everything into barrels in the back of his pickup truck.

After sifting through it all to remove inedible materials, the pig farmer would cook the rest in a big pot over an open fire. The resulting "slop" wasn't appetizing to look at but was eagerly devoured by the pigs. Local farmers added *honohono* grass to the mixture.

Most household food waste goes into the garbage disposal these days, and the rest of it gets bagged and tossed out with the trash. However, both Derek and Jason report that their supermarkets and restaurants, respectively, still segregate their food wastes for pickup by local pig farmers. The farmers still cook the slop and feed the pigs with it, Derek notes, "And then we end up buying our pork from them!"

fishponds played in the ancient Hawaiians' ability to maintain a sustainable ocean food source.

"Kona kampachi is flying off the buffet and is also selling well on our à la carte menu," Jason reports. "We use it to replace the frozen red snapper. It's like night and day. We notice that people fill up their plates and bring them back clean. That helps us a lot because there's a lot less wastage."

Pagoda: New Twist on an Old Favorite

Some might consider the buffet itself a dinosaur in today's dining culture. Jason disagrees. "Change is necessary," he contends. "Customers' palates have to change so it becomes more a matter of quality rather than quantity. The objective shouldn't just be about finding the cheapest all-you-can-eat alternative." Rather, the appeal should lie in a wide variety of foods, available all at once—a large-scale version of the plantation lunch-hour cornucopia of offerings, if you will.

"You just have to watch one of these banquet parties," he explains, "to see that it's all about family celebrations and an opportunity for folks to bond. It's an Island thing and it would be a shame if it were lost because we went strictly with an à la carte menu. We plan on developing a brand new buffet concept, including individually plated portions of food that are nicely presented rather than simply put out there in a chafing dish. It's possible to put out a new style of buffet that combines the best of old and new."

These are challenges that confront many young chefs today. "You have to continue to grow and evolve, while staying connected to the past because you have that older crowd," Jason admits. "The pressure is to make it perfect."

Feeding Family Connections

If Jason ever needed to be reminded as to how the old and new sometimes merge into a single reality, all he has to do is look across the Pagoda dining room and see his father and his father's friend, Charlie

Artisanal products on the rise: chocolate, cheese and bread.

Higa—the co-founder of Hawai'i's iconic Zippy's Restaurant chain—enjoying their oxtail soup.

"They're here at least once a week, every week," Jason says. "Whenever I think of traditional local dishes, oxtails always pop up in my mind. I used to take my grandparents to Zippy's all the time. Grandpa loved oxtail. Later, he got sick and was confined to the hospital for a couple of years. During that time, I would pick my grandma up every day and we would take him lunch. He passed away while I was working on the Mainland. I had just started a new job and wasn't able to get back. I've always regretted that he never got to try my food as a trained and experienced chef."

You can't throw a stick in Hawai'i without hitting a dish that someone treasures not solely for its flavors, but for its place in family lore. If he were alive, Jason's grandfather would surely enjoy Jason's spin on his favorite oxtails. In preparing the cut, Jason demands that the meat is cooked well, but not overcooked. "You want it tender, but still connected to the bone," he insists. Jason's demanding standards gave birth to his popular Kim Chee Oxtail Fried Rice. (See page 80 for the recipe.)

Makeovers, Not Leftovers

"Fried rice makes me think of one of Derek Kurisu's favorite sayings, 'Makeovers, not leftovers,'" Jason muses. "It's his spin on not wasting food. When people don't have much, they get very creative in coming up with ways to stretch what they have in order to feed themselves and their families. The older generation, Derek says, were masters at this!" The principle of not wasting food is one of those old-time values that remain intensely relevant today. While it might appear at first glance that restaurants are bastions of extravagance and waste, the reality is that ingredients—especially good ingredients—are very expensive, and success in the restaurant business depends on reducing waste. On a daily basis, chefs have to come up with specials by evaluating what ingredients they have on hand. "We have to move certain items," Jason explains. "It's a matter of economics." For example, after the prime filets of meat and fish are used in certain dishes, the rest is ground to make sausages, burgers or meatballs. Bones are boiled for stock.

Likewise, in Hawai'i's plantation days, every part of an animal was used. Nothing was wasted—the

31

Homemade pickles, jams and jellies form part of the backbone of food traditions bridging Then and Now.

bones and less-than-premium parts often ending up in soups and stews. Fish, too, was eaten head and all. Even vegetables were used in totality, including stems and leaves. These practices have not changed all that much over time, although perhaps today it's more often a professional chef who bears the burden of innovating "makeovers," rather than the home cook.

Adhering to Derek's makeover mantra—and Hawai'i's multiethnic traditions—Jason has come up with an array of dishes that make use of scraps to create something elegant and delicious, such as Kalbi Potstickers, Braised Short Rib Ravioli, Seared 'Ahi Poke, and Prime Rib Chili. Blackened *ahi sashimi* can be turned into 'ahi burgers and the leg meat from the lobster pinched out to make ravioli.

"We have a cook who takes scraps of chicken and salmon belly to make delicious employee meals," Jason marvels. "He feeds eight others that way. My wife and I do it at home, too. We buy the whole chicken instead of just parts. That way we can carve out the breast meat, make chicken salad sandwiches and use the rest for stew, and throw the bones in a pot to make soup. We can easily make three or four meals from one chicken." Families without professional cooks in the house and who are pinched for time snap up grocery-store whole rotisserie chickens for the same purpose.

Catching Up? Or Ahead of the Game?

"The local palate has come a long way over the last 10 years," Jason notes. "People appreciate food a lot more now, and they appreciate the effort it takes to make something look and taste perfect. Farmers are growing a greater variety of produce, so chefs have more and more local ingredients to choose from."

There are certain techniques that have been popular in certain Mainland urban centers for years that just didn't catch on in the Islands, or are just coming around now. Some of these fall under the banner of "molecular gastronomy," including foams, spherification, gelification and emulsification. Hawai'i chefs are utilizing more of these techniques, Jason notes, if not as widely as their Mainland counterparts.

"Cooking comes down to technique and balance," he says. "It doesn't have to be 'crazy-kine' innovation. It can be more simple—comfort foodish, even—but it has to be done right, like grilling a steak perfectly. Or, take *kabocha* (Japanese pumpkin)—roasting it gives it a completely different flavor than boiling it. Rather than flavoring the kabocha by adding shoyu and sugar, the roasted kabocha itself will add flavor to your dish."

Younger chefs can't settle for doing the same things that chefs did 20 years ago and still be successful, Jason points out. "We try to manipulate food using more locally grown ingredients in an effort to attract new customers while also keeping the regulars coming back for more." Today, Jason and other influential Gen-X chefs are making their mark in the continuing evolution of Hawai'i Regional Cuisine. "We push the ingredients and we push each other to be better. You have to change and adapt if you want people to keep coming."

Jason enjoys the challenge of refining his creative edge. Today, one of his favorite food events is the annual Taste of the Hawaiian Range event on Hawai'i Island, which showcases grass-fed Island beef. The 30 invited chefs are assigned various parts of the animal to prepare, including specialty cuts like tongue, ear, feet, tail, tripe and even mountain oysters. "It's fun," Jason says. "It tests your creativity and we chefs get a rare opportunity to hang out, talk story and compare notes." It's a creative challenge very reminiscent of the Black Box parties Jason that enjoyed in California. And it's exciting to see modern eaters explore—for fun—cuts of meat their grandparents or great-grandparents ate out of necessity.

When it's all said and done, good food is good food. It might be easy to discount the kau kau prepared by past generations as simple comfort food, a sort of common denominator that was dictated largely by availability and cost. If so, it should be considered to be the *highest* rather than *lowest* common denominator—the best of all worlds.

Whether someone knows what the fancy French term *"terroir"* means or not (it's the way the special characteristics of an area give a food its unique qualities), consider that coffee produced in Kona and Ka'ū on the Big Island are and have been judged the finest in the world for a very long time. Or consider that *"umami,"* humankind's widely accepted "fifth flavor," only relatively recently identified, long existed in the flavors of incomparable dishes from years past such as hekka, *nishime*, *oden* and the savory depths of noodle broth.

After all, the chef's challenge since time immemorial has been to make the best of what he or she had. This mission remains today: to create, to satisfy, to inspire, to soothe, to entertain, to excite, to please, to amuse, to celebrate, to nurture and to connect. Such is the power of food.

Food festivals like Kā'anapali Fresh on Maui celebrate the bounty Hawai'i has to offer.

Fresh, local vegetables—an important part of cooking both Then and Now.

Part Three

Island Cooking Then and Now

The recipes found on the following pages are paired together—one Then dish from Derek Kurisu, a classic plantation or traditional local-style favorite, followed by a Now dish from Chef Jason Takemura, a reinterpretation or contemporary presentation. Each pairing is connected in some way: an ingredient, cooking technique, ethnic origin, flavoring agent or basic underlying concept. (A few of these recipes blur that line—technological advances like the microwave speed up preparation of Derek's meals, for instance, and some dishes that haven't changed much are still served in Jason's restaurants today.)

Both men emphasize the simplicity inherent in traditional Hawai'i cooking—fresh ingredients, basic preparations—making these 62 dishes ones that the average home cook can easily replicate.

A note regarding the recipes from Derek: Although amounts are listed as accurately as possible, it's important to understand that in the old days food was usually prepared *oyoso*, a Japanese word meaning "approximately" or "more or less." Cooking was done to taste and adjustments were constantly being made on the fly. How many people are we feeding? Two? Five? Ten? No problem. You simply stretched what you had and never wasted anything. Recipe yields, therefore, are approximate or, in some cases, nonexistent—make as much or as little as you desire.

To create a complete meal, serve dishes with rice (of course!) and perhaps a salad or pickled veggies on the side (see page 152 and 154 for recipes). Or, pick a few favorites and serve them pūpū-style at your next family gathering.

I grew up in a plantation community with lots of Filipino friends and neighbors. At a party once, I noticed the host had added fried potatoes to the adobo and they really absorbed all the great flavors of the dish. I thought it was so good that I've incorporated potatoes into my recipe ever since. I also like to sear or fry the meat and potatoes before serving, for the added texture and flavor that the carmelization creates. Locals call this "koge," or slightly burnt. I always joke that stoves back then only had "medium" and "high" settings. There was no such thing as "low." The idea was to cook fast. -DK

3 to 4 pounds chicken thighs (or pork shoulder)
2 to 3 pieces garlic, crushed
12 whole peppercorns
3 bay leaves
1 tablespoon Hawaiian salt
2 to 3 tablespoons patis (Filipino fish sauce)
½ cup cider vinegar
½ cup water
3 potatoes
Cooking oil

Cut meat into bite-sized pieces. Combine all ingredients except for potatoes in a deep pot. Bring to a boil and simmer with cover slightly open.

Pierce each washed potato a few times with a fork then cook in a microwave for 5 minutes. Rinse under running water and remove skins. Cut into 1- to 2-inch thick slices and fry in oil.

Add potatoes to the other ingredients when about half to two-thirds of the liquid has boiled off.

The adobo is done when the meat is fork-tender and nearly all the liquid has boiled off. If desired, add a bit of oil and brown the meat once the liquid has cooked off.

Serves 10 to 12.

Garlic Lemongrass Pork

1½ pounds pork tenderloin, sliced ¼-inch thick
3 tablespoons cooking oil
2 tablespoons chopped lemongrass
2 tablespoons chopped garlic
1 large onion, thinly sliced
2 stalks celery, thinly sliced
10 cherry tomatoes, halved
½ cup sliced green onions
¼ cup chopped cilantro

Pork Marinade

¼ cup chopped garlic
2 tablespoons finely chopped lemongrass
½ cup fish sauce
½ cup sugar
½ cup lemon juice
2 pieces chopped Hawaiian chili pepper (or to taste)

Combine marinade ingredients and marinate pork for 3 to 4 hours. In a very hot skillet or wok, add oil, then sauté onions and celery for 1 minute. Add chopped garlic and lemongrass and sauté for another 30 seconds to 1 minute. Add marinated pork and sauté until it is just cooked through. Finish by adding the tomatoes, green onions and cilantro.

Serves 4.

This dish reflects my love for Thai food. When I was the executive chef at Chai's Island Bistro, we didn't serve traditional Thai food, but more of a Pac-Rim style that included some Thai influences. Being in the kitchen with Chef Chai, who is from Thailand himself, gave me the opportunity to pick up some of his style and techniques. This dish is my take on something that Chai might have whipped up as an employee meal for us. -JT

Whenever you had a get-together on the plantation, you were sure to find a hot wok somewhere nearby and chicken hekka would just sort of "happen." In those days, people would pick their own takenoko (bamboo shoots) and cut up a whole chicken and use all of it—that's the true hekka. Now days, takenoko (along with the other traditional vegetables) comes in cans and we go to the store and buy just the chicken breast or thigh meat—most of it is even boneless and skinless! Some people use sake to enhance their chicken hekka, but I like to use butter for that little extra "oompha." -DK

6 dried shiitake mushrooms
2 pounds boneless chicken, cut into bite-size pieces
1 14-ounce can chicken broth
3 slices fresh ginger
½ cup shoyu
½ cup sugar
2 8.75-ounce cans sukiyaki no tomo (sukiyaki vegetables)
1 carrot, thinly sliced
1 round onion, thinly sliced
1 teaspoon salt
¼ cup sake
2 tablespoons butter
1 bunch green onions, chopped
Cooking oil

Soak dried shiitake mushrooms in chicken broth. When rehydrated, reserve broth and slice mushrooms. Fry chicken pieces together with ginger slices in pot with a little cooking oil. Mix together shoyu and sugar. Add to chicken, along with sukiyaki no tomo. Add reserved chicken broth and remaining ingredients through butter. Simmer until chicken is cooked through. Sprinkle green onions over hekka before serving.

Serves 6 to 8.

Shabu Shabu

1 small head won bok, cut lengthwise into 2-inch pieces
4 pieces baby bok choy or choy sum, cut into 2-inch pieces
1 onion, julienned ¼-inch thick
6 fresh shiitake mushrooms, sliced
½ block medium-firm tofu, cut into ½-inch cubes
4 ounces enoki mushrooms
8 ounces fresh salmon, sliced into 8 pieces
¾ pound rib-eye steak, sliced paper-thin
8 medium shrimp, peeled and deveined; reserve shells for Shabu Shabu Broth (recipe follows)
Chicken and Tofu Dumplings (recipe follows)
Shabu Shabu Broth (recipe follows)
Ponzu Dipping Sauce (recipe follows)

Using a portable burner, bring Shabu Shabu Broth to a simmer at the dining table. Add ingredients to the hot broth a few at a time. Be sure to cook dumplings for at least 3 to 4 minutes to ensure that the raw chicken has completely cooked through before eating. Serve with dipping sauce on the side.

Serves 4 to 6.

Ponzu Dipping Sauce

1 2-inch piece konbu (dried seaweed)
1 cup bonito flakes
1 cup shoyu
¾ cup yuzu (Japanese citrus) juice
⅓ cup mirin (Japanese cooking wine)
3 teaspoons sugar
2 teaspoons rice vinegar

Combine all ingredients in a pot and bring to a simmer. Once it begins to simmer, remove from heat. Let cool, then strain.

Shabu Shabu Broth

1 stalk lemon grass
6 cups chicken stock
3 tablespoons mirin (Japanese rice cooking wine)
2 tablespoons shoyu
Shells from 8 medium shrimp
3 whole dried shiitake mushrooms, rehydrated and excess water squeezed out
1 4-inch piece konbu (dried seaweed)

Crush lemongrass to break up the fibers. Combine all ingredients in a pot and bring to a low simmer for 15 minutes. Strain, keeping only the broth. Can be prepared up to a day before serving.

Beyond being convenient, one of the benefits of one-pot cooking is that it brings the flavors of all the ingredients together in a tasty blend. The term "umami" is inspired by the savory goodness of this type of cooking. Old-time dishes like chicken hekka (see previous page), nishime and oden are examples of that. Today, one of our favorite family dinners is shabu shabu. We use a flavorful broth, salmon and lots of veggies to reduce fat and make for a more healthy meal. If you ask my daughter what she wants to eat for dinner, I bet she'll say, "Shabu shabu!" -JT

Chicken and Tofu Dumplings

½ block medium-firm tofu
8 ounces ground chicken breast
1½ tablespoons oyster sauce
1 teaspoon sesame oil
1 egg
2 tablespoons chopped cilantro
2 tablespoons sliced green onions
Gyoza (potsticker) wrappers
1 egg yolk

In a bowl, mix first 7 ingredients until well incorporated. Lay gyoza wrappers on a clean cutting board. Spoon 2 teaspoons of filling onto each wrapper. Brush egg yolk onto the edge of half each wrapper. Fold in half and press firmly to seal.

Makes 20 to 25 dumplings.

Once, I prepared this Korean Chicken at a TV show taping where I cooked with a Korean chef, the dad of the owners of the popular Café Duck Butt. He looked at me and said, "Well, maybe the chef that created it was Korean, so that's why they call it 'Korean Chicken'—but it's not from Korea." So maybe Korean Chicken is kind of a new thing. All I know is that it's so popular it's helped to drive up the cost of the drumettes! –DK

Korean Chicken

2 pounds chicken
   mix of drumettes and boneless chicken thighs
½ cup flour
½ cup shoyu
½ cup sugar
5 cloves garlic, crushed or minced
1 to 2 teaspoons ko choo jang sauce
   (Korean chili pepper paste)
1 tablespoon sesame oil
1 teaspoon roasted sesame seeds
¼ cup chopped green onions
Cooking oil, for frying

Pat chicken pieces dry, coat with flour and fry. Rest fried chicken on a rack over paper towels to drain excess oil. Combine shoyu, sugar, garlic, ko choo jang sauce, sesame oil, sesame seeds, and green onions in a bowl. Dip chicken pieces in marinade mixture and serve.

Combine ingredients in a sauce pan and bring to a simmer. Thicken to desired consistency with cornstarch slurry (2 tablespoons cornstarch mixed with 1 tablespoon cold water; use as much as needed).

Serves 4 to 6.

Garlic Shichimi Chicken

1½ pounds boneless chicken thighs, roughly cubed into 2-inch pieces
1 tablespoon minced garlic
2 teaspoons kosher salt
1 egg, whisked
6 tablespoons potato starch
Garlic Chicken Sauce (recipe follows)
Cooking oil, for frying

Mix chicken, garlic and salt together well and marinate for 2 to 4 hours. After marinating, coat chicken with egg and potato starch.

Preheat deep fryer (or deep pot with oil) to 350°F. Gently slide chicken pieces into the hot oil, being sure to separate them so that they cook evenly and don't stick together. Cook in small batches to avoid lowering the oil temperature. This ensures that your chicken will be crispy, not soggy and greasy.

Cook until chicken is cooked through and crispy. Drain excess oil and place in a clean heatproof bowl. Immediately toss with just enough Garlic Chicken Sauce to coat. For best results, cook just before eating.

Serves 4.

Garlic Chicken Sauce

2 cups water
2 cups white sugar
½ cup shoyu (Yamasa brand preferred)
½ cup minced garlic
2 teaspoons shichimi togarashi
    (Japanese "seven-flavor chili pepper" spice)

Combine ingredients in a sauce pan and bring to a simmer. Thicken to desired consistency with cornstarch slurry (2 tablespoons cornstarch mixed with 1 tablespoon cold water; use as much as needed).

Everybody has their own version of Korean Chicken—a chicken wings-and-drumettes sort of dish. In the restaurant, we wanted something boneless. The shichimi togarashi *is an ideal spice for this because it gives the dish a little hint of heat, but not as hot as cayenne pepper. This has become one of the signature items on the Pagoda menu. -JT*

Miso Pork

This is an Okinawan-inspired dish, because Okinawans like to use miso in their cooking. Miso is a good marinade because it is healthy and helps tenderize the pork. One word of caution, however: You've got to watch out because miso is very sensitive to high heat and it will burn! So, don't be cooking with miso and go wandering off somewhere to talk-story and goof-off. -DK

3 pound boneless pork shoulder roast
½ cup miso
½ cup shoyu
⅓ cup sugar
2 cloves garlic, crushed
2 cups water
1 small finger of ginger, crushed

Slice the pork into 2-inch thick strips. In a large pot, combine miso, shoyu, sugar, garlic and water; mix into a smooth sauce. Add ginger and pork. Cover and bring to a boil. Turn down heat and let simmer for 2½ to 3 hours or until tender. Keep heat low and stir every ½ hour or so to ensure the miso doesn't burn. If desired, transfer to a sauté pan and brown the outside of the pork, being careful not to burn the miso sauce. Shred or slice pork to serve.

Serves 6 to 8.

Kim Chee–Smoked Pork

1½ cups shoyu
¾ cup sugar
¼ cup Kim Chee Base (see recipe, page 154)
2 pounds boneless pork butt, cut into 2-inch wide pieces
2 pounds applewood chips, for smoking
1 tablespoon vegetable oil
2 medium onions, julienned
1 cup sliced green onions
Red chili pepper flakes, to taste
Salt and pepper, to taste
4 tablespoons guava jelly
1 cup green onions

Combine shoyu, sugar and Kim Chee Base and marinate pork for at least 4 to 8 hours. Overnight would be ideal. Preheat smoker to 180°F and presoak applewood chips in water for at least 20 minutes. Smoke pork for 4 hours. When cool, slice crosswise into ⅛-inch thick pieces.

In a very hot skillet or wok, heat vegetable oil. Add sliced pork and sauté. Add onions and season with salt, pepper and chili flakes. Add guava jelly and mix well. The jelly will melt, coating the pork; allow it to caramelize. Finish with green onions and serve hot. Garnish with kim chee, if desired.

Serves 8 to 10.

Anybody who knows me knows how much I love smoking food. It's been my main hobby and I make good use of my smoker at home to smoke tako, pork, fish, whatever! One of our favorite recipes was Smoked Pork and Onions. Through a friend, we learned to do the smoked pork with guava jelly, which adds sweetness. Now that we had the salty and the sweet going, we needed the spicy to complete the balance. At the Hukilau, we used to have a dishwasher who was from Korea. She taught us how to make traditional-style kim chee, and that's what I settled on to incorporate heat into the recipe. -JT

Shoyu Pork

5 pounds pork belly
   (or boneless pork shoulder roast, cut in half)
1 cup shoyu
1 cup sugar
1 cup pineapple juice
5 slices fresh ginger

In a deep pot, cover pork with water and boil for 1 hour. Discard water and rinse pork. Slice pork into 2-inch pieces and, in the same pot, combine with remaining ingredients. Bring to a boil and continue to simmer, about 45 minutes, until tender.

Serves 8 to 10.

I remember my family receiving pork from the "buta kau kau man" who would come to neighborhood homes and pick up slop once or twice a week (see page 30). In return, he would periodically bring everybody a piece of pork as a way of saying thanks. That pork was so good—I really looked forward to it! To this day, I love local pork, which is leaner and more flavorful than Mainland pork. This is another recipe I learned from my buddy, George Yoshida. Here on the Big Island, a lot of our plantations grew sugar. But on the other islands, they grew a lot of pineapple. The flavor goes well with pork, so we often use it for cooking with ham or spare ribs. I like to use it for shoyu pork—with the shoyu, it makes a unique flavor and the juice helps tenderize the pork. -DK

Braised Pork Belly Bao Bun "Sliders"

2 pounds pork belly, skin removed
Pork Marinade (recipe follows)
4 tablespoons hoisin sauce
2 teaspoons sriracha (or other hot sauce)
½ cup Kim Chee, chopped (see recipe, page 154)
1 cup thinly sliced won bok
½ cup finely julienned Fuji apple
½ cup julienned green onions (reserve bottoms and stems for marinade)
12 fresh bao buns, steamed and warmed

Pork Marinade

1½ cups shoyu
1 cup sugar
½ cup water
2 pieces star anise
1 3-inch piece ginger
4 stalks green onion, white part only
5 cloves garlic, whole
Pinch crushed red chili flakes

Cut pork belly into a 2-inch by 2-inch by 8-inch block. Combine marinade ingredients and marinate pork overnight (8 to 12 hours), turning the pork over every 4 hours.

Preheat oven to 325°F. Transfer pork and marinade into an oven-safe pan. Cover pan with foil. Place in the oven and braise for 3 hours. Remove from oven, remove foil and allow to cool, with the braising liquid, before refrigerating until ready to use. Remove cold pork from the liquid and slice crosswise ¼-inch thick. Reserve braising liquid.

In a sauce pan, heat sliced pork belly in the reserved braising liquid. Mix hoisin and sriracha together and set aside. In a separate bowl, mix won bok, apples and chopped kim chee together. Spread 1 teaspoon of hoisin-sriracha sauce in each warm, softened bao bun. Place 2 to 3 slices of pork per bun, topped with the kim chee slaw.

Garnish with green onions.

Makes 12 sliders.

Growing up in Hawai'i, everybody loves to eat manapua. They're sort of like SPAM® musubi—the kind of grab-and-go food perfect for a snack or quick meal. Instead of serving plain manapua in the restaurant, we put this spin on the classic Island favorite. We started with some of the Asian ingredients and flavors that I learned at Chai's and adapted them to our needs and tastes. The secret is our braised pork, which goes really well with the bao buns. Sliders are really popular these days—no need to cut them in half or anything, they're all individual servings. -JT

This is one of those classic plantation dishes utilizing canned goods, comparable perhaps to modern convenience foods like frozen TV dinners. Many plantation homes, like my family's, didn't have large freezers, so canned goods were the thing—they're fully cooked and will last forever in the can. Especially when there's a shipping strike or threat of natural disaster, local families still stock up on toilet paper, rice and canned goods. Plus, Pork and Beans has gravy, so you can stretch it and eat it over rice. It's so easy to prepare that even plantation men could make Pork and Beans with Vienna Sausage—they just had to heat 'em up. -DK

Pork and Beans *with Vienna Sausage*

2 15-ounce cans Pork and Beans
   (Van Camp's brand preferred)
1 4.6-ounce can Vienna sausage

Cut Vienna sausage into 1/3 inch-thick "coins." Heat Pork and Beans in a saucepan over medium heat. Add sausage and bring to nearly boiling (you should see a few bubbles slowly break the surface). Stir and serve.

Serves 4.

Hukilau's Famous Prime Rib Chili and Rice

⅔ pound pancetta, small diced
2 onions
4 cloves garlic
3 pounds prime rib, diced
3 cups tomato sauce
1½ 12-ounce bottles dark beer
2 ⅔ cups beef stock
2 teaspoons chili powder
4 teaspoons cumin
4 teaspoons cocoa powder
1½ teaspoons oregano
1 teaspoon cayenne pepper
1½ teaspoons coriander
3 bay leaves
Salt and pepper, to taste
2½ pounds kidney beans
Chili pepper flakes, to taste

In a large, heavy-bottomed pot over medium-high heat, sauté pancetta until fat is rendered out and pancetta is crispy. Do not drain the fat. Add onions and sweat for 5 minutes. Add garlic and sauté for 3 minutes. Add all remaining ingredients except for the kidney beans and chili pepper flakes. Season with salt and pepper to taste. Bring to a boil, then reduce to a simmer. Simmer for 45 minutes. Add the kidney beans and continue to simmer 15 minutes longer. Taste and adjust seasoning. Add chili flakes for desired spiciness. Serve over hot rice.

Serves 8.

We do prime rib at both the Hukilau and the Pagoda. We also slice up some of the meat to make prime rib sandwiches. However, we're still always left with the end cuts and the chain area (the lip on the ribeye). The chain has a lot of flavor because of its fat content and the seasoning that's contained there. That all becomes the ground beef in the chili. My chili is influenced by the time I spent working in California, where there was a strong Mexican influence on the food. They like to incorporate chocolate into their recipes, like in their molés (sauces). The cocoa powder adds richness, a slight bitterness and depth to the chili. We also use a dark beer instead of water in our chili, which adds further flavor and helps to round everything out, too. -JT

Teriyaki Beef

1 pound beef, thinly sliced
   (may also use pork or chicken)
1 cup shoyu
1 cup sugar
4 tablespoons ketchup
2 tablespoons oyster sauce
1 1-inch piece ginger, crushed or sliced
3 cloves garlic, crushed

Combine all ingredients, except meat, and mix. Soak meat in marinade
for at least 30 minutes. Grill or pan fry.

Serves 4.

Teriyaki meat is an old-time favorite. It's based on the
standard shoyu-sugar-ginger-garlic flavor base. To add a
little bit of a twist to my teri beef, I put a little ketchup
in it. The story behind that goes back some 50 or 60 years,
when KTA sponsored a contest to see who could make the best
teriyaki sauce. I was just a kid at the time, but I learned
how to make the winning sauce recipe when I started working
at the store in high school. My job was to mix the marinade,
which included ketchup, oyster sauce and, back then,
Diamond Shoyu—a brand that's no longer around. Every shoyu
is different, so no matter what brand you use, you'll have to
adjust it to fit your taste. Over the years, I've adjusted
and modified this sauce, but it's still based on that old KTA
contest recipe. —DK

KAU KAU

Kalbi Potstickers

¼ pound choi sum
½ teaspoon sesame oil
1 tablespoon oyster sauce
1 teaspoon toasted sesame seeds
4 fresh shiitake mushrooms
½ pound cooked Kalbi (see recipe, page 84)
Gyoza (potsticker) wrappers
1 egg yolk
2 tablespoons vegetable oil
2 tablespoons water
Ponzu Dipping Sauce (see recipe, page 44)

In salted boiling water, quickly blanch choi sum for 30 seconds, remove from pot and immediately plunge into iced water to stop cooking. Once cooled, gently squeeze out excess water. Finely chop the choi sum and place in a small mixing bowl. Add sesame oil, sesame seeds and oyster sauce and toss together.

Chop shiitake mushrooms and dice kalbi into ¼-inch cubes. Add the mushrooms and kalbi to choi sum and mix together.

On a clean cutting board, lay out the gyoza wrappers. Place 2 teaspoons of kalbi filling in the center of each wrapper. Brush along the edges with the egg yolk, fold in half and press firmly to seal. Stand filled potstickers upright, sealed edges pointing up, and press gently to flatten out the bottoms.

Heat 2 tablespoons of vegetable oil over medium heat in a nonstick pan. Place potstickers flat side down in the oil. Cook for 2 minutes to sear to a golden brown. Very carefully, add 2 tablespoons of water to the pan and cover immediately with a tight-fitting lid, steaming the potstickers. After 2 minutes, remove the cover; continue to cook until the remaining water evaporates out. Serve immediately with dipping sauce.

Makes 12 to 15 potstickers.

Much of what we do at the restaurant has to do with eliminating food wastage. A lot of planning and creative thinking goes into menu planning to avoid waste, but since we cook a lot of food for banquets, we still end up with leftovers—food that was prepared, but never served. The best way to make use of all of it is to run pūpū specials, like potstickers. The ingredients in this recipe combine a lot of classic Korean flavors—it's like a Korean mixed-plate in one little wrapper.   -JT

To be honest, you could say that the Portuguese Sausage-Hamburger patty featured in this recipe was a happy accident. I went to do a cooking gig across town and forgot to bring some of the ingredients I needed for hamburger patties. On the spot, I figured I could use chopped-up Portuguese sausage in place of the ground pork that I usually put into the patties and hamburger buns to replace the missing bread crumbs. I've been doing it that way ever since. It even simplifies things because the Portuguese sausage acts like a seasoning. Instead of buying all sorts of herbs and spices, you use something that already has an interesting flavor. I also use a white gravy on this, which not everyone does. -DK

Loco Moco

with Portuguese
Sausage-Hamburger Patty

Portuguese Sausage-Hamburger Patty (recipe follows)
Egg (see Note)
Cooked rice
White Gravy (recipe follows)

Portion out rice into a bowl or onto a plate. Top with a hamburger patty, fried egg and gravy.

Note: A loco moco is traditionally served with an over-easy or sunny side up egg. Raw or undercooked eggs carry a risk of food poisoning, so we recommend serving this dish with a fried egg instead.

Serves 1.

Portuguese Sausage-Hamburger Patties

1 10-ounce package Portuguese sausage
1 pound local grass-fed ground beef
½ cup sliced round onions
1 egg
1 slice bread, crumbled
Oil, for frying

Remove Portuguese sausage from casing and rough chop into small pieces (approximately ½-inch chunks). Mix with ground beef, onions, egg and bread crumbs. Form into patties and pan fry. Reserve pan (and remaining drippings) for making gravy.

Makes 6 to 8 patties.

White Gravy

1 14.5-ounce can chicken broth
¼ cup flour
Black pepper

Combine flour with 1 cup of chicken broth. Whisk together, removing all lumps, and set aside. On medium heat, in the same pan used to fry the hamburger patties, add the remaining chicken broth. Scrape the bottom and sides of the pan with a wooden spoon to remove the browned bits. Add black pepper to taste, stir and bring to almost a boil. Slowly add the flour-broth mixture, stirring well, until gravy reaches desired thickness.

Sake–Soy-Braised Short Rib Loco Moco

1 cup cooked rice
1 piece of Sake–Soy-Braised Short Rib (recipe follows)
1½ cups braising liquid (reserved from Short Ribs)
2 eggs, cooked to your preference

In a sauce pan, reduce braising liquid down to ¾ cup. Mound the rice in the center of a large bowl. Using the back of the rice paddle, gently pat the rice down to create a flat surface. Place the short rib on the rice, followed by the reduced braising liquid. Place eggs on top.

Serves 1.

Sake–Soy-Braised Short Ribs

2 pounds boneless beef short ribs, cut into 8-ounce pieces
2 onions, halved
2 carrots, peeled
1½ cups apple juice
1 cup shoyu
1 cup sake
1 cup mirin (Japanese cooking wine)

½ cup sugar
2 tablespoons sesame oil
8 cloves garlic
1 bay leaf
1½ cups water
Salt and pepper, to taste
Cooking oil, for searing meat

Season short ribs with salt and pepper and heat oil in a heavy-bottomed braising pan. Sear meat on all sides until caramelized. Remove from pan and add onions and carrots. Stir-fry briefly. Add meat back to the pan and add the remaining ingredients. Bring to a boil then reduce to a simmer. Cover with foil. Braise for 3 hours, skimming the grease from the top every ½ hour. Remove the meat from the pan and strain the liquid into a clean container. Let the grease rise to the top and skim off. Pour the hot liquid back over the meat and allow to cool. Do not discard braising liquid.

Makes enough for 4 Loco Mocos.

Both the Hukilau and Pagoda are known for doing their own versions of Hawaiian comfort food. The original Hukilau restaurant was established in San Francisco by a small group of Hawai'i folks who had moved to the Mainland and missed the local food that reminded them of home. This dish takes loco moco to a different level, using the Sake–Soy-Braised Short Ribs we offer as an entrée on our night menu. To add a different twist to it, we use apple juice as a sweetener, cooking it down to add depth to the flavor. -JT

Canned corned beef is one of those plantation staples that can be cooked in many different ways. Corned Beef Hash Patties and Corned Beef with Cabbage are probably the local top two. Both feature ingredients (potatoes and cabbage) that are reasonably priced, so you could always put plenty of "filler" to stretch the hash and feed more people. People like canned corn beef because it has a lot of flavor and it's "bulletproof" for home cooks because it doesn't require a lot on your part. Today, corned beef hash patties are mainly served as a breakfast dish with eggs. However, they used to be eaten as a dinner entrée with rice. And ketchup—lots of ketchup. -DK

Canned Corned Beef Hash Patties

2 large potatoes
1 12-ounce can corned beef
1 egg
½ teaspoon pepper
½ teaspoon garlic powder
2 teaspoons vegetable oil
½ cup flour

Boil potatoes until fork-tender. Remove skin and smash into chunks. In a bowl, combine potatoes, corned beef, eggs, pepper and garlic powder. Form into patties.

Coat with flour and fry.

Serves 2 to 3.

Corned Beef Hash Patties

1 pound cooked Corned Beef (recipe follows), chopped fine
1 pound of frozen shredded hash brown potatoes (not patties)
1 pound potatoes, ½-inch dice, boiled until fork tender
1 cup chopped green onion
1 teaspoon kosher salt
½ teaspoon black pepper
½ teaspoon garlic powder
½ teaspoon onion powder
Vegetable oil, for frying

Combine all ingredients while potatoes are still frozen and form into 1 cup portions, flattened into patties. In a nonstick pan, on medium-high heat, add 1 teaspoon of vegetable oil. Cook patties for 2 minutes on each side.

Serves 10.

Corned Beef

1 quart water
1½ cup kosher salt
2 teaspoons pink curing salt
1 cup brown sugar
3 quarts iced water, including ice
3 bottles dark lager beer
4 bay leaves, crushed
2 teaspoons granulated garlic
2 teaspoons juniper berries
2 teaspoons black peppercorn
1 4-pound whole beef brisket,
    fat trimmed to ¼-inch

Brisket Rub

2 teaspoons mustard seeds
2 teaspoons whole black peppercorn
2 bay leaves

Bring 1 quart of water to a simmer. Add salts and sugar and simmer until dissolved. Add the iced water, seasonings and 1 bottle of beer. In a large container, brine the brisket in the refrigerator for 10 days. Remove from brining liquid and rinse very well in cold water.

Preheat oven to 300°F. Season with rub ingredients. Place brined brisket in a deep, oven-safe roasting pan. Pour 2 bottles of beer over the meat and cover with aluminum foil. Place in oven and cook for 3 to 4 hours (depending on thickness of meat). When done, remove foil cover and let cool in the juices.

This is our take on a breakfast classic. We start by making our own corned beef with Big Island grass-fed beef, which has a specific flavor to it. We brine it for 10 days, then beer-braise it with a dark beer in the oven for three to four hours. The inspiration for the corned beef actually started from pastrami—we wanted to make our own in-house and realized the same process could also make corned beef. It's taken lots of experimentation, trial and error and making adjustments to the process over a period of several months to get it just right. -JT

Goteborg sausage was popular on the plantations because it was cheap and very tasty. It's always been one of my favorites ever since I was a little kid. Everybody used to fry them up and pack it along on picnics, in their kau kau tins (lunch pails used by plantation workers) and even for dinner. Like chorizo, Goteborg was so packed with flavor that it went great with rice. Even if you had just a little, you could eat it with plenty of rice and get full. I'm not quite sure why Goteborg remains so popular in Hawai'i—especially Kaua'i, which must be No. 1 in per capita consumption in the country! -DK

Goteborg "UFOs"

Goteborg sausage (summer sausage)
Cooked rice
Nori goma furikake
    (seaweed and sesame seed rice topping)

Slice sausage thinly, $\frac{1}{8}$-to $\frac{1}{4}$-inch thick, and pan-fry. The edges of each
slice should curl up, forming a bowl-like shape. When the sausage is
cooked to your liking, remove from pan and drain on paper towels.

Heap 2 to 3 tablespoons of rice in each sausage "bowl." Sprinkle
approximately $\frac{1}{8}$ teaspoon of furikake on each.

New York Steak with Hāmākua Aliʻi Mushroom and Truffle–Edamame Cream Risotto

½ cup edamame (soybeans), shelled, divided
1 tablespoon heavy cream
2 teaspoons truffle oil
¼ cup sliced Hāmākua Aliʻi (king oyster) mushrooms
½ teaspoon chopped garlic
½ cup uncooked Arborio rice
3 tablespoons white wine

6 cups chicken stock, hot
1 tablespoon butter
Salt and pepper
12-ounce New York strip steak
Kosher salt
Vegetable oil

In salted water, boil ¼ cup edamame for 2 minutes. Strain and immediately transfer edamame to a bowl of iced water. This will stop the cooking process. When cooled, strain again and transfer to a blender. Add heavy cream and truffle oil. Season with salt and pepper, then purée. Set aside.

In a large, heavy-bottomed sauce pan add 2 tablespoons of vegetable oil. Over high heat, sauté the mushrooms until caramelized. Once caramelized, season with salt and pepper, add garlic and cook until garlic is fragrant and lightly browned. Remove mushrooms and garlic from the pan and set aside. Using the same pan, add raw rice and 2 teaspoons of vegetable oil. Sauté, constantly moving the pan, being sure to coat each grain of rice with oil. This will give the rice a nutty flavor. Deglaze the pan with white wine. Using a wooden spoon, continue stirring the rice. Once the wine has cooked out, add 1 cup of stock and continue stirring. When nearly all the stock has been absorbed, add another cup of stock. Continue this process and keep stirring until the rice is almost al dente. This should take about 15 minutes. You may need more stock, or you might not need it all. Every batch is a little different. When the rice is cooked, add the mushrooms back to the pan with ¼ cup edamame. Add the Truffle–Edamame Cream and butter. Continue stirring. The final product will have a porridge-like consistency. Season with salt and pepper.

Season steak liberally with kosher salt and pepper on both sides. Sear the steak over high heat in a heavy-bottomed pan with 1 tablespoon of vegetable oil. Do not move the meat while it cooks. This will help to give it a nice crusty sear on the outside. Cook for 2 to 3 minutes on each side. For medium-rare, remove from the pan immediately. For medium or well-done steak, place the pan in the oven at 400°F and cook to desired doneness. Let steak rest on a cutting board for 5 minutes before slicing. Serve over the risotto.

Serves 2.

This is a classic play on the simple-but-delicious pūlehu (grilled) steak and rice. In Hawaiʻi, we love to pair any sort of meat with rice. Of course, in a restaurant, you've got to kick it up a bit, which is how we arrived at this dish. -JT

Oxtail Stew

Oxtails are one of those special foods that seem to be more popular in Hawai'i than they are anywhere else in the country. In the past, oxtails were reasonably priced. All of a sudden, however, it seems the cut has exploded in popularity (and price) and is being used in so many ways. I like to use oxtails in beef stew. It works out great, because it adds a whole different dimension to the stew. It is more flavorful and way more interesting. It's a satisfying feeling to suck the meat and collagen right off the bone. -DK

1 medium round onion
4 stalks celery
2 potatoes, peeled
3 carrots, peeled
2 tablespoons cooking oil
2 to 3 pounds oxtail pieces, cut between the joints
2 tablespoons flour
1 46-ounce can V8 juice
Hawaiian salt
Pepper
Sugar

Chop vegetables into 1- to 2-inch pieces. Heat cooking oil in a deep pot. Coat oxtail pieces in flour and brown on all sides. Add onions to the pot and cover with V8 juice. Simmer for 1½ hours, then add remaining vegetables. The liquid in the pot should just barely cover the vegetables. Add water as needed. Simmer for another hour or until oxtail is tender. Add Hawaiian salt, pepper and sugar to season to taste. Serve over rice.

Serves 4 to 6.

Kim Chee–Oxtail Fried Rice

3 cups day-old cooked rice
4 tablespoons Stir Fry Sauce (recipe follows)
1½ tablespoons reserved bacon fat or cooking oil
¼ cup diced round onion
½ cup cooked oxtail, taken off of the bone and shredded
¼ cup Kim Chee, chopped (see recipe, page 154)
¼ cup chopped green onions
Salt and pepper

In a mixing bowl, gently break up the rice and separate the grains. Be careful not to mash the rice. Add the Stir Fry Sauce and mix together so that each grain is lightly coated.

In a nonstick pan over medium-high heat, add the bacon fat and round onions. Sweat the onions until translucent. Do not brown them; they should remain the same color. Add the rice and sauté. Add oxtail and kim chee to heat through. Add green onions and remove from heat. Taste and season, if needed, just before serving.

Serves 2 as an entrée.

Stir Fry Sauce

½ cup sugar
1¼ cup shoyu
¼ cup sambal oelek (garlic chili sauce)
1½ cups sesame oil
3 cups oyster sauce

Combine all ingredients, mix well and refrigerate. This is a good all-purpose sauce for stir-frying meats and vegetables and adding flavor to other dishes.

The origin of this dish goes back to one evening at the Hukilau, when an employee accidently overcooked an entire pot of oxtails. The meat was already falling off of the bone, and you can't serve that dish like that. "What am I going to do?" I thought. I decided to combine the meat from the oxtail with the kim chee one of our employees had taught us to make and create a fried rice dish. I took what I had and turned it into our special for the evening. It was our bestseller that night and has remained on the menu ever since. -JT

Batayaki is a great dish, especially if you have guests over, because everybody cooks their own food. You can prepare everything before the guests arrive and you don't have to slave over the stove all day. It's a great concept because you can talk story, enjoy a drink and have a nice time with each other over a meal. It's the kind of activity that really brings people together. Plus, everybody has a choice—they cook what they want to eat—so nothing is wasted. This is one of my wife, Georgeanne's, and my son, Blake's, favorites. The problem is, for them, I still have to prepare it AND cook it! -DK

Butter
Zucchini, sliced
Eggplant, sliced
Hāmākua Aliʻi (king oyster) mushrooms
Chinese cabbage, chopped
Bean sprouts
Boneless beef, pork or chicken, thinly sliced
Shrimp or scallops
Salmon or ʻahi belly

If using salmon or ʻahi belly, brine fish for 20 minutes in 2 tablespoons of Hawaiian salt and 4 cups water. Heat a frying pan and add butter. Fry ingredients in butter to desired doneness. Serve with Batayaki Dipping Sauce (recipe follows).

Batayaki Dipping Sauce

1 lemon, juiced
¼ cup shoyu
1 tablespoon ko choo jang sauce (Korean chili pepper paste)
1 tablespoon sesame oil
1 cup chicken broth (or half of a 14-ounce can)
¼ cup grated daikon
2 tablespoons chopped green onions

Combine ingredients through chicken broth. Mix well, then add grated daikon and chopped green onions.

KAU KAU

Sizzling Kalbi

3 pounds beef short ribs, sliced ¾-inch thick
4 cups shoyu
1½ cups sugar
1 cup ko choo jang sauce (Korean chili pepper paste)
½ cup chopped green onion
2 tablespoons fresh ginger pieces
1 tablespoon chopped garlic
2 teaspoons sesame oil
2 tablespoons toasted sesame seeds
¾ cup Kim Chee (see recipe, page 154)
1½ cups shredded cabbage
1 onion, julienned
3 tablespoons butter

Special tools: Cast iron sizzle platter(s) or cast iron flat-top grill pan.

In a large bowl or plastic bag, combine first 9 ingredients (through sesame seeds). Mix together thoroughly to coat meat. Marinate short ribs for 24 hours. After marinating, grill short ribs until cooked rare on an outdoor grill over high heat. Set aside for 3 minutes to rest. Cut short ribs into 2-inch slices.

Heat a cast iron sizzle platter over high heat for about 3 to 5 minutes until it starts to smoke. Mix together cabbage and onions and divide into 3 portions. Place 1 portion of cabbage and onions, along with 1 tablespoon of butter, on the hot platter. Immediately add 1 pound of sliced kalbi on top of the cabbage, followed by a portion of kim chee. The meat will continue to cook slowly to desired doneness. Repeat the process with remaining meat and vegetables.

You may want to use more than one sizzle platter, in order to serve the meat on the platter at the table, or use a large flat-top grill pan of the type that stretches across two stove burners to cook larger batches.

Serves 8.

Growing up, one of my favorite family dinners was batayaki (see previous page). That was an occasion when the whole family got together, cooked together and enjoyed a nice, relaxed dinner. This dish features classic kalbi—just beefed up, you might say. The cabbage isn't just for filler or decoration—it keeps the meat from contacting the hot platter directly, which would really overcook it. I recommend ordering the dish medium-rare because no matter what, the meat does continue to cook on the platter. It's the garlic butter that actually hits the platter and gives the dish its spectacular sizzle, pop and irresistible aroma, which reminds me of batayaki.
-JT

EAFOOD
seafood
seafood
SEAFO
SEAFOOD
SEAFOOD
SEAFOO
SEAFOOD
SEAFOOD
od
food
SEAFOOD
SEA

You'll notice this recipe makes use of a microwave oven. Obviously, this is not something that was available back in the real "old days," but I think this recipe is true to the spirit of old-style cooking because it is fast and simple. Anybody can do it. As the dish cooks, the moisture from the fish and cabbage seeps out and melds together with the seasonings to create a great, flavorful sauce. If you can't get a whole fish, you can use fish fillets.*

Steamed Chinese-Style Whole Fish

1 small or ½ large Chinese cabbage
1 2-pound whole fish (moi, 'ōpakapaka, uhu, snapper or mullet), cleaned
3 cloves garlic, minced
1 2-inch piece ginger, skin removed, minced
2 tablespoons chung choi (salted pickled turnip), washed and minced
2 tablespoons dried Chinese black beans, rinsed
⅓ cup peanut oil
5 stalks Chinese parsley, optional
¼ cup shoyu

Wash and slice cabbage leaves into 1- to 2-inch strips. Fill a large microwave-safe dish almost to the top with cabbage. Make two diagonal slashes on each side of the fish and lay it over the cabbage. Mix together minced garlic, ginger, chung choi and Chinese black beans. Spread half of the mixture inside the fish cavity and the other half over the fish.* Cover dish with microwaveable plastic wrap and microwave on high for 8 to 10 minutes. The size of the fish and microwave power will vary the cooking time. The center of fish should be cooked through.

While fish is cooking, heat peanut oil in a small pan over high heat until it begins to smoke. Top cooked fish with Chinese parsley and shoyu. Slowly pour hot oil over fish.

Serves 4.

* If you are using fillets, spread half the seasoning mixture onto the cabbage, directly under the fish, and the other half on top of the fish.

Whole Steamed Hawaiian Kampachi

1 2-pound whole Hawaiian kampachi, cleaned, gutted and scaled
1 3-inch piece of fresh ginger, peeled, and julienned
1 cup sliced fresh shiitake mushrooms
3 tablespoons sake
3 tablespoons oyster sauce
2 teaspoons sesame oil
2 teaspoons sugar
3 teaspoons shoyu
1 teaspoon garlic chili paste (optional)
¼ cup sliced green onions
¼ cup chopped cilantro
6 tablespoons peanut oil (or vegetable oil)

Score the kampachi on both sides with 2-inch by 2-inch diamonds, down to the bone. Scatter ginger and shiitake mushrooms over fish. In a pan that will fit into your steamer, lay fish on its side.

In a bowl, mix together sake, oyster sauce, sesame oil, sugar, shoyu and chili paste. Pour over the ginger and mushrooms. Cover the pan and steam for 15 to 18 minutes. If you don't have a steamer, you can use an oven-safe pan, cover with foil and bake at 325°F for 15 to 20 minutes. After the fish is cooked through, carefully remove the foil; the steam will be very hot and can burn you.

Using two spatulas, one at the head and one at the tail end, carefully remove the fish and transfer to a serving platter. Pour all of the remaining juices from the pan over the fish. In a small sauce pan, heat the oil over medium high heat. When it begins to smoke, remove it from the heat. Spread green onions and cilantro on top of the fish. Slowly pour the hot oil over to release the flavors.

Serves 2 to 4, depending on fish size.

Growing up in Hawai'i, one of our favorite activities was spearfishing. One of my best memories was taking a whole fish—like an uhu (parrot fish)—stuffing it, wrapping it in foil, pouring beer inside and then steaming it on the grill. Today, we use Hawaiian kampachi, which is a great fish that is farmed off of the Kona coast of the Big Island. -JT

Hilo has its own unique surimi, which is a seasoned, raw whitefish paste. In fact, people like to buy surimi in Hilo and take it to the other islands either for themselves or as omiyage (gifts).

I think surimi is a perfect vehicle to implement the philosophy of "makeovers, not leftovers," because you can mix just about anything you have with the surimi. No matter what you do with it, it's going to taste good. You can even use okara (soybean pulp). In this recipe, I put in poke and an egg. Ever notice when you buy poke, you usually eat about half and you don't know what to do with the rest of it? Mixing it with the surimi turns the leftover poke into a completely different dish. It's tender inside and crispy outside. -DK

Surimi and Poke Patties

1 pound surimi (raw fish paste)
½ to ¾ pounds poke, your favorite style
1 egg
Water chestnuts, diced (optional; amount to taste)
Cooking oil, for frying

Mix surimi and poke. Add egg. Mix and set aside in refrigerator for 5 minutes. Heat oil in frying pan. Form mixture into 2-inch balls and flatten into patties. Fry patties in hot oil until golden-brown and crisp on the outside.

Makes 20 to 25 patties.

Note: Surimi can be found in Asian markets or in Hawai'i grocery stores in the seafood section. Some stores sell it in plastic tubs, and others sell it by the pound in plastic-wrapped trays. On the Mainland, imitation crab is sometimes called surimi. This product has already been cooked and cannot be used for this recipe.

Shiitake Mushroom and Spinach Dynamite-Crusted Opah

4 shiitake mushrooms, julienned
1 cup packed fresh spinach
4 teaspoons mayonnaise
1½ teaspoons sesame oil
2 teaspoons tobiko
Dash of cayenne pepper
2 6- to 8-ounce portions of opah (moonfish) fillet
Salt and pepper
Vegetable oil, for sautéing

In a sauté pan on medium-high heat, sauté mushrooms in vegetable oil. Season with salt and pepper. When mushrooms are cooked, add spinach, season again with salt and pepper, and cook until spinach is wilted. Remove from heat, transfer to a plate and cool.

Preheat oven to broil setting. In a mixing bowl, combine cooled mushroom mixture, mayonnaise, sesame oil, tobiko and cayenne.

Season opah fillets with salt and pepper on both sides. In a nonstick pan on medium-high heat, sear the opah for 2 minutes on each side. Transfer to an oven-safe pan. Top fish with dynamite mix. Broil for about 2 to 3 minutes, until it is caramelized and crusty.

Serves 2.

I love going to sushi bars. Most places these days have a version of what's known as a "dynamite" sushi roll, which features a mayonnaise base. Our goal with this dish was to take that flavor profile and transform it into an entrée, adding vegetables and mushrooms to the dish. By covering the fish all over and then broiling it in the oven, we added a textural element—a nice crust— to it, as well as the caramelized flavor. By baking a fish with mayo, you retain the moisture in there, so it's tender on the inside and crusty on the outside. -JT

This is a simple and delicious way of preparing shrimp. One summer, I prepared it for the students at a local youth academy. After the event had passed, I received a phone call from the grandmother of one of the students. She said, "My granddaughter loved the shrimp so much that she wanted to prepare it for dinner for the whole family." They did and everyone enjoyed it. It made me so happy that the young girl wanted to do that for her whole family. I always think about that story whenever I make this dish. -DK

Broiled Shrimp

White shrimp or black tiger prawns (21-25 size)
Mayonnaise
Garlic powder
Paprika

Devein the shrimp. If you wish, you can butterfly them. This may make them easier to serve. Season shrimp with garlic powder. Spread a teaspoon of mayonnaise on each shrimp. Top with a sprinkle of paprika. Place shrimp on foil-lined baking sheet and broil until mayonnaise darkens and shrimp is opaque (approximately 3 to 6 minutes depending on your broiler).

Shrimp and Shiitake Mushroom Potstickers

3 pounds tail-off shrimp, peeled and deveined
7 shiitake mushrooms
1 tablespoon black pepper
1 tablespoon granulated garlic
1 teaspoon onion powder
1 egg
1 egg white

3 tablespoons oyster sauce
1 teaspoon salt
½ cup chopped green onion
¼ cup chopped cilantro
Gyoza (potsticker) wrappers
1 egg yolk

Place all of the filling ingredients into a food processor and pulse until mixed well. On a clean cutting board, lay out the gyoza wrappers. Place 2 teaspoons of filling in the center of each wrapper. Brush along the edges with egg yolk, fold in half and press firmly to seal.

Preheat deep fryer to 350˚F. Fry the pot stickers until golden brown. Serve with Miso Yuzu Butter (recipe follows) as a dipping sauce.

Makes 40 to 50 potstickers.

Miso Yuzu Butter

½ small Maui onion, sliced
2 teaspoons shiro miso (white miso paste)
¼ cup sake
¼ cup white wine
1½ tablespoons mirin (Japanese cooking wine)

1 teaspoon chopped ginger
2 teaspoons Stir Fry Sauce (see recipe, page 80)
½ cup heavy cream
½ tablespoon yuzu (Japanese citrus) juice
3 tablespoons cold butter

In a sauce pan add the first 6 ingredients and simmer until reduced by half. Add the Stir Fry Sauce and heavy cream. Reduce by half again. Add the yuzu juice and remove immediately from the heat. Finish by adding the butter and whisking until it is completely incorporated. Strain and serve.

Any time I eat ramen noodles, I'll always order some potstickers to go with it. Potstickers are easy to make. The most common ones use pork and vegetables, but this is a different twist. It's perfect as an appetizer or side dish. -JT

Tako Poke

½ pound cooked tako (octopus), sliced
3 tablespoons sugar
1 tablespoon minced ginger
½ teaspoon chili pepper (fresh minced or dried flakes), optional
3 tablespoons shoyu
1 tablespoon chopped green onions

In a bowl, spinkle sugar over tako and let stand for 1 minute. Add ginger, chili pepper (if using), shoyu and green onions. Mix and serve.

While attending the University of Hawai'i at Mānoa, I worked as a fish cutter at Times Supermarket in Honolulu. That was back around 1972 to '73. I learned a lot working there, including how to make poke—'ahi poke, tako (octopus) poke, all kinds of poke. After I returned to Hilo, I started making poke at KTA. The trick to making good tako poke is to put the sugar in first and rub it in. That marinates the tako and makes it softer. Then, you add lots of finely sliced ginger, chili pepper for a little heat and finally the green onions and shoyu. It's really simple. -DK

KAU KAU

Spicy Smoked-Tako Poke

3 pounds fresh local tako (octopus), cleaned, beak removed
3 tablespoons Hawaiian salt
¼ cup mayonnaise
2 tablespoons sesame oil
Pinch of cayenne
1 cup Maui onion, julienned
½ cup sliced green onion
¼ cup tobiko
Salt and pepper

Set smoker with kiawe wood to 180°F. Season the tako with Hawaiian salt. Smoke for about 2 to 2½ hours. After it is cooked through, remove from the smoker and allow to cool. Once cooled, slice the tako into ½-inch pieces.

In a mixing bowl, add the tako, followed the remaining ingredients. Fold together gently. Taste and season again with salt and pepper if needed.

Makes approximately 2½ pounds of poke, enough for 10 to 15 people, served pūpū-style.

Cuisine

If I haven't mentioned it before, I love my smoker! We smoke all of our meats and seafood ourselves. Drinkers know that smoked tako tastes good by itself and goes really well with beer, but it can get dry. In a restaurant, every dish has to be able to stand on its own, so we mixed the smoked tako with other elements to create something moist and flavorful. The mayo, onions and tobiko all serve specific functions, adding moisture and a nice little crunch to the dish. -JT

When it came to fishing, diving, catching frogs or prawns, nobody came close to "Uncle Tada" Hamane. He even made me a spear so I could go with him to the river to catch prawns. He was so good at it that he would easily bag more than everyone else combined. Then, we would go to his house where he taught me how to cook the prawns using this exact recipe. He would always remind me, "Make sure you cut off the whiskers 'cause it going tickle your throat." It's so simple, seasoned with only garlic powder, salt and paprika, then fried in peanut oil. However, I still think it's the absolute best way to eat prawns or any kind of head-on shrimp—can't mess with perfection! -DK

Uncle Tada's Fried Prawns

5 prawns, butterflied
Garlic salt
Paprika
1 tablespoon peanut oil

Sprinkle garlic salt and paprika over prawns. Fry in peanut oil until prawns are opaque and shells turn red-orange.

Optional: Use head-on prawns for extra "local flavor."

Garlic Salt-and-Pepper Shrimp

2 tablespoons vegetable oil
¼ cup chopped garlic
2 red jalapeño peppers, seeds removed and julienned (optional)
¼ cup sliced green onion
1 cup all-purpose flour
1 cup cornstarch
1 pound fresh Kauaʻi head-on shrimp
2 tablespoons of Garlic Seasoning (recipe follows)

Garlic Seasoning

1 tablespoon granulated garlic
1 tablespoon fine sea salt
2 teaspoons sugar
¼ teaspoon white pepper

Preheat fryer to 360°F. In a wok or large sauté pan, over medium-high heat, add vegetable oil. Add garlic and sauté until golden-brown and it begins to slightly crisp. Add the red jalapeños and green onion. Sauté for about another 30 seconds.

Combine flour and cornstarch in a bowl. Dredge the shrimp in the flour mixture. Shake off all the excess flour and deep-fry for about 2 minutes until crispy and golden-brown. Immediately after removing the shrimp from the fryer, add the shrimp to the pan with the garlic–jalapeño mix and season with 2 tablespoons of Garlic Seasoning. Toss everything together. It may seem like you are adding a lot of seasoning to the shrimp, but the mix is well-balanced and you shouldn't find it too salty.

I've always loved head-on shrimp. Well, to be honest, everything I make reflects the way I like to eat. But who can resist shell-on, head-on, crispy, eat-the-whole-thing shrimp? You get all kinds of flavors you don't get when you eat cooked shrimp without the shell. Also, you don't end up stuck in the kitchen peeling a whole pile of shrimp! -JT

Local people have many different ways to prepare fish with mayonnaise because it keeps it nice and moist. When we were kids, we used to always mix mayonnaise and shoyu together. You might say it was our "universal dressing" for fish, vegetables—just about anything. Following that concept, I simply added some garlic powder and thinly sliced lemon. The result reminds me of those flavors from the past and it goes really well with the fish. -DK

Baked Salmon

1 pound salmon fillet
½ teaspoon garlic powder
2 tablespoons mayonnaise
¼ cup fresh lemon, thinly sliced
2 teaspoons shoyu

Preheat broiler. Place salmon fillet on a sheet of aluminum foil large enough to create a loose packet around the fish. Sprinkle fillet with garlic powder. Mix shoyu and mayonnaise together and spread on salmon. Top with lemon slices. Broil for 2 minutes or until mayonnaise browns. Bring sides of the foil sheet up and loosely enclose salmon. Bake for 8 minutes at 345°F for approximately 5 minutes. Check for desired doneness.

Serves 2.

Blackened-Salmon Salad

1 4-inch piece hasu (lotus root), peeled
6-ounce fillet fresh salmon (skin-on, optional)
1 teaspoon Blackening Spice (recipe follows)
2 ounces fresh, local mixed greens
1 tablespoon diced cucumber

1 tablespoon diced tomato
2 tablespoons Ponzu Vinaigrette (recipe follows)
Salt and pepper
Vegetable oil, for deep-frying and pan-searing

Preheat fryer or deep pot with cooking oil to 350°F. Use a mandolin slicer to slice hasu root into ⅛-inch thick pieces. Carefully slide the slices into the fryer one at a time to ensure that they do not stick together. Fry for about 1 to 2 minutes, until very light golden-brown. Remove from oil and drain on a paper towel. Lightly season with salt and pepper. Set aside.

Season the salmon with salt and pepper on one side only (skin-side, if you have left the skin on). Season the opposite side with Blackening Spice. In a hot nonstick pan on medium-high heat, using 1 tablespoon of vegetable oil, sear the Blackening Spice side first. Cook for about 1 minute—take care not to burn the spices as it will create a bitter flavor. Gently flip the fish over and cook for another 2 minutes (total cooking time will depend on the thickness of the fillet). Fish should be cooked to medium doneness.

In a mixing bowl, toss the greens, cucumbers and tomatoes with the Ponzu Vinaigrette. Serve the salmon blackened side up, atop the greens, with the hasu chips around the edges of the dish. This will keep the chips crispy, rather than mixing them into the greens where they will get soggy.

Serves 1.

Ponzu Vinaigrette

6 tablespoons shoyu
½ cup rice vinegar
2 lemons, juiced
1 tablespoons yuzu (Japanese citrus) juice

½ cup brown sugar
1 tablespoon sesame seeds, toasted
½ cup salad oil

In a mixing bowl, whisk together all ingredients except for salad oil. Slowly add oil while continuing to whisk.

Makes 2 cups.

Besides cooking what I want to eat, I also like cooking my wife's and daughter's favorites. When we met, my wife didn't eat fish. When she was pregnant, however, her doctor suggested that she eat salmon for the Omega 3 fatty acids. The Blackening Spice I use is made up of more than 12 different spices, including sugar to balance out the heat. We only season one side of the fish—more would be overkill. The lemon and vinaigrette dressing also help to tone down the heat. We serve the salmon over 'Nalo Greens and use hasu chips instead of croutons. This is now one of my wife's favorite dishes. -JT

Blackening Spice

¼ cup shichimi togarashi
    (Japanese "seven-flavor chili pepper" spice)
3 teaspoons sugar
1 teaspoon black pepper
2 teaspoons salt
1 teaspoon onion powder
1 teaspoon garlic powder
½ teaspoon cayenne pepper
½ teaspoon oregano
¼ teaspoon dried thyme

Mix all ingredients together.

Makes 6 tablespoons.

Sardines and Onions

1 can sardines
½ round onion, sliced
1 teaspoon sugar
1 tablespoon shoyu

Empty contents of can (including the liquid) into a frying pan. Fry together with sliced onion. When onions turn soft and translucent and fish is heated through, add sugar and shoyu. Stir together, taking care not to break the sardines apart too much. Serve sardines topped with onions and sauce.

Serves 1 as a meal over rice, or several as a pūpū dish.

Canned sardines used to be really, really cheap during plantation days—maybe 10 cans for a dollar or even 12 for a dollar. Some people don't like the smell of sardines, but I've always loved them cooked with shoyu, sugar and onions. When I was little, we lived together in the same house with my grandparents and aunt. I remember one day my aunty was cooking sardines and onions. I got so excited that I ran to the park to tell my brother to come home because we were going to have sardines and onions. I got scolded for shouting it out so loudly for everyone to hear. After all, it was just poor man's food, but I loved it that much! Today, there are all kinds of sardines and they all go well with onions. I like the smoked ones the best. —DK

Pan-Roasted Kampachi

2 6-ounce fillets Hawaiian kampachi, with skin on
1 cup won bok, sliced 2-inch thick
2 cups baby bok choy, sliced 2-inch thick
½ red bell pepper, julienned ¼-inch thick
2 tablespoons Stir Fry Sauce (see recipe, page 80)

¼ cup Yuzu Butter Sauce (recipe follows)
2 teaspoons Wasabi Oil (recipe follows)
Salt and pepper
Vegetable oil

With a sharp knife, lightly score 1-inch diamonds into the skin of the kampachi. Take care not to cut into the flesh of the fish. Season the kampachi on both sides with salt and pepper. Preheat oven to 350°F. Over high heat, add 1 tablespoon of vegetable oil to a hot, oven-safe, nonstick pan. Gently lay the fish in the pan, skin-side down. Do not move the fish while it cooks. Sear for about 2 minutes, then transfer the pan to the oven for about 3 minutes (a thicker fillet may need more time). Flip fish over and continue cooking in the oven for another minute. Remove from oven and transfer to a serving platter, skin-side up.

In a clean pan, heat 2 teaspoons of vegetable oil on medium-high heat. Add won bok, baby bok choy and red bell pepper. Season with salt and pepper. Add Stir Fry Sauce and sauté for 1 to 2 minutes.

Pour Yuzu Butter Sauce and Wasabi Oil on the plate alongside the fish. Serve with rice or other starch.

Serves 2.

Wasabi Oil

¼ cup grapeseed oil (or vegetable oil)
1 tablespoon rehydrated wasabi powder
1 stalk green onion, cut into 2-inch lengths

Combine all ingredients in a blender on high speed. Blend for about 1 minute. Strain through a cheese cloth slowly, ensuring that no particles come through the cloth.

Makes ¼ cup.

Yuzu Butter Sauce

1 shallot, finely chopped
¼ teaspoon grated ginger
3 tablespoons sake
1 teaspoon oyster sauce
2 tablespoons heavy cream
2 teaspoons yuzu (Japanese citrus) juice
2 tablespoons cold butter
Salt and pepper

In a small sauce pan, add shallots, ginger, sake and reduce until liquid is almost completely evaporated. Add oyster sauce and cream and cook until reduced by half. Remove from heat and add yuzu juice and butter. Whisk continuously until butter is emulsified into the sauce. Season with salt and pepper.

Makes ¼ cup.

When I was a kid, my dad and grandpa liked fishing out at Barber's Point. On the way home, everyone would stop at my parents' house for dinner and my grandma would fry up the fresh fish we had caught, like pāpio *(young trevally or jackfish) and* āholehole *(young Hawaiian flagtail). Later on, we got a boat and also caught* ta'ape *(blueline snapper),* moi *(threadfin) and* nabeta *(razor wrasse). Because of this, I love head-on pan-fried fish. Not everyone likes to deal with all those bones, though, so we serve fillets in the restaurant to make it easier to eat. Still, with the skin on, it reminds me of how my grandma would prepare the fish.* -JT

My dad was a good 'opihi picker. In fact, he had a reputation as the "'Opihi Man." He would go along the Hakalau coastline, right outside of Kolekole Park, with his buddy, Alan Takeya, who was also an excellent 'opihi man. I remember my father wore special tabi (footwear) that my grandmother made out of scrap pieces of cloth. And, since my father was a machinist at the suga mill, he had a special knife that he made out of stainless steel to scrape the 'opihi off the rocks. He never took me or my brothers along, though, because he said we were too slow and woul probably get knocked into the ocean by the waves. My job was to shell all the 'opihi that he brought home so he could give them to his friends for pūpū. Actually, there was always so much 'opihi at our house that we sort of took it for granted. It was better to share them with others because it was such a special delicacy! -DK

'Opihi Two Ways

Salt and Pepper Style

'Opihi
Hawaiian salt
Hawaiian chili pepper or red pepper flakes
Ogo (seaweed), chopped

> Shuck opihi with a spoon by scraping the meat off the shell. Rinse under water and add seasonings to taste.

Grilled with Shoyu

The larger 'opihi (far left) is great for grilling.

'Opihi
Shoyu
Hot sauce

> Place 'opihi on the grill or on a baking rack in an oven, shell-side down. Pour shoyu and hot sauce over the 'opihi. They are ready to eat when the sides of the 'opihi loosen from the shell (about 3 to 4 minutes). Be careful not to spill the sauce when removing from the grill.

Baked Oysters with Bacon–Creamed Spinach and Truffle Hollandaise

4 raw oysters on the half shell
8 teaspoons Bacon–Creamed Spinach (recipe follows)
4 teaspoons Truffle Hollandaise (recipe follows)
1 teaspoon tobiko (flying fish roe)

Preheat broiler. Top oysters with 2 teaspoons Creamed Spinach each and broil for 3 minutes. Spoon 1 teaspoon of Truffle Hollandaise over spinach. Top each oyster with ¼ teaspoon tobiko.

Bacon–Creamed Spinach

1 slice raw bacon, chopped
1 small shallot, minced
2 tablespoons white wine
¼ cup heavy cream
1 cup fresh spinach, packed
Salt and pepper

Truffle Hollandaise

4 teaspoons Hollandaise Sauce (see recipe, page 174)
½ teaspoon white truffle oil

Whisk together.

Add bacon to a small, cold sauce pan with 2 teaspoons of cold water. Turn stove to medium-high heat. (Starting the bacon in a cold pan will cause it to render out its fat. If you start it in a hot pan, it will sear in the fat.)

As the bacon cooks, the fat will render out and the water will evaporate out. This will provide the "oil" to cook and sauté in. When the bacon begins to crisp, carefully spoon out half of the oil (save for another use, such as Kim Chee–Oxtail Fried Rice, page 80). Add the shallots and sweat. After a couple of minutes, the shallots should be translucent with no color. Add white wine and reduce until almost completely evaporated. Add cream and spinach. Season lightly with salt and pepper. Continue to cook until the liquid released by the spinach reduces down to about 2 tablespoons. Remove from heat and season again with salt and pepper to taste.

Raw oysters are great, but we can't just sell raw oysters in our restaurant—they don't move fast enough. If you've got oysters, you need to have a second preparation in mind so they don't go to waste. So, this is my own twist to the classic Oysters Rockefeller dish, with bacon, cream sauce and tobiko for texture. -JT

Raw Crab Poke

Like 'opihi, raw crab has always been a big part of Hawaiian food. You often see it served at lū'au and such. Beforetime (in the old days), we used to catch 'a'ama crab (black rock crab) on the rocks and pickle and eat them, but it's getting harder and harder to get 'a'ama crab. Folks just don't go out to catch them, I guess. Now, I use blue pincher crabs or white crab, which comes clean and frozen at many markets. -DK

1 pound raw blue pincher or white crab
2 tablespoons Hawaiian salt
½ teaspoon chili pepper flakes
1 teaspoon 'inamona (roasted kuku'i nut), optional
2 tablespoons chopped ogo (seaweed), optional

Lift the shell from the back of the crab leaving the front of the crab attached. Cut each crab in half, remove gills and rinse. Add Hawaiian salt, chili pepper flakes and, if using, 'inamona and ogo. Refrigerate for at least 30 minutes before serving.

Black Bean Kona Crab with Hāmākua Mushrooms and Truffle Butter

2 whole Kona crabs
1 cup flour
1 cup cornstarch
Garlic Seasoning (see recipe, page 106)
2 tablespoons softened butter
1 teaspoon white truffle oil
1 cup sliced Hāmākua Ali'i (king oyster) mushrooms
1 small Maui onion, julienned

2 tablespoons chopped garlic
2 tablespoons sake or white wine
1 cup Black Bean Sauce (recipe follows)
½ cup diced tomatoes
¼ cup sliced green onion
¼ cup chopped cilantro
Vegetable oil, for deep-frying and sautéing

Preheat deep fryer to 350°F. Remove back shell from crab and clean out gills. Remove legs and set aside. Cut the bodies into 2-inch chunks (you can usually get 4 to 6 pieces per crab). Mix together flour and corn starch. Dredge crab pieces (including legs) in flour mix. Shake off excess flour. Deep-fry for 3 to 4 minutes, or until golden brown and crispy. Remove from oil, drain and immediately season well with Garlic Seasoning. Set aside.

In a mixing bowl, whip together softened butter and truffle oil with a whisk. Set aside.

Heat 2 tablespoons of vegetable oil in a large, heavy sauté pan on medium-high heat. Sauté mushrooms, season with salt and pepper. Once the mushrooms are cooked, add Maui onions and garlic. Continue cooking for 2 to 3 minutes. Deglaze pan with sake. Add Black Bean Sauce and bring to a simmer. Finish by adding the fried crab pieces, tomatoes, green onion, cilantro and truffle butter. Mix well and serve immediately.

Serves 2 to 4.

Kona crab is prized for its sweet, delicate taste, which makes it ideal to take on the flavors of other ingredients. This dish utilizes Hāmākua mushrooms, black bean sauce and truffle butter. I'm not sure how I started experimenting with truffles and black beans, but the combination is very good. The two are completely different— one European, the other Asian. The sweetness of one balances the saltiness of the other. If you can't get Kona crab, you can use spanner crab, which is the same species, or, in a real pinch, even Dungeness crab would do. -JT

Black Bean Sauce

¼ cup fermented salted black beans
1 tablespoon vegetable oil
1 tablespoon garlic
1 tablespoon chopped ginger
¼ cup sake
2 tablespoons oyster sauce
1 cup chicken stock
1½ tablespoons sugar
1½ tablespoons cornstarch
2 tablespoons cold water

Soak black beans in cold water for 5 minutes, changing out the water every minute. Drain and set aside. Heat 1 tablespoon of vegetable oil in a sauce pan on medium heat. Sauté garlic and ginger for 2 minutes. Add black beans and sauté for another 2 minutes. Deglaze pan with sake. Add oyster sauce, chicken stock and sugar. Simmer for 10 minutes. Mix cornstarch and water together and use to thicken sauce to desired consistency.

SIDES AND SPECIALTIES

Warabi (fiddlehead fern) shoots used to grow wild in the rural areas of every island. It seemed to be especially plentiful on the Big Island. It's not like they grew on anyone's property, it was everyone's property—on the hillsides, up in the mountain, along river banks. You'd just go and pick 'em, take 'em home, wash 'em and eat 'em. You still find patches of warabi all over the place here on the Big Island. For me, it's something I learned about a little later in life. When I was small, we used to eat more kakuma (see page 152) than warabi. Now, warabi is really popular. It's sold at many farmers markets and even in some supermarkets. -DK

Warabi and Pork

10 stalks of warabi (fiddlehead fern)
¼ pound ground pork
½ round onion, sliced
2 tablespoons sugar
2 tablespoons shoyu
Salt and pepper to taste
1 tablespoon cooking oil

Wash, clean and cut warabi into 1-inch lengths. Parboil warabi for
approximately 1 minute in well-salted water. Rinse, drain and set
aside.

Heat oil in a sauté pan and stir-fry pork and onion slices. When pork
is browned and onions have softened, add warabi pieces and briefly
stir-fry together. Mix sugar and shoyu together in a small bowl and
add to pan. Stir together and cover. Allow to simmer for about 10 to 15
minutes, until warabi is limp and a dull, olive-green color. Serve with
rice.

Serves 2 to 4.

Forest to Table

Warabi

"Today, foraging is getting popular again, but in the past, it was more of a necessity. Everyone had limited incomes, so everybody had to live off the land to some extent just to put food on the table," Derek explains. "Growing up, we didn't think it was anything special to eat stuff that we harvested in the wild, like warabi (pohole, hōʻiʻo or fiddlehead fern), kakuma (Hawaiian tree fern) or takenoko (bamboo shoots). In fact, we probably wished we had a nice steak or something instead. Today, however, I often wish I could eat some of those nostalgic foods from the past—things that our parents, grandparents, uncles, aunties and friends would go out and gather."

Throughout his youth, it seemed that nature's pantry would always remain stocked, Derek notes. For various reasons, however, everything has gotten harder to find. In part, hoarding or overharvesting contributed to the depletion of some foods. Also, back then, no matter if the properties were owned by the plantation or some government entity, they were treated as public lands. "Anyone could go and pick stuff," Derek says. Since then, however, large tracts of these once wild or unclaimed lands have been developed into homesteads or subdivisions. And, since the closure of the plantations, former sugar lands have been sold to private owners who have fenced off the old network of plantation roads heading mauka, barring access to the upland forests and river gulches where these edible plants thrived.

Not all foods were totally wild, however. In fact, if you check back far enough, some of these plants were cultivated at one point in time. A watercress patch or bamboo grove, for example, did not spontaneously sprout from the earth. Rather, they were likely to be associated with a family or camp that was once situated there. A solitary wī apple, avocado, ʻulu (breadfruit), persimmon, orange or mountain apple tree were other indicators of some human history.

"Those were the days," Derek recalls, "when people used to share what they had, especially if they had extra of something. It's kind of amazing that we were able to experience that kind of environment and saw it slowly disappear." The plants still grow wild, but not too many people know where and when to go to gather them efficiently, much less how to prepare them. And although you can sometimes find fresh warabi in the supermarket or takenoko in cans at the Asian grocery, kakuma is one of those foraged foods that just isn't for sale at any store. The appetite and know-how for some of these items from our past is vanishing.

"We're fortunate to have seen the transition between the two worlds," Derek says. "Change is not bad, but there are some things from the past that are worth preserving. If it's possible, I'd like to take some of the values, such as respect, from the past and plant them in the future—respect for the land and for people."

Takenoko

Kakuma

Smoked Pork and Warabi Salad

1 cup smoked pork, sliced ⅛-in thick (see recipe, page 52)
3 cups warabi, cut into 2-inch lengths
½ cup Maui onion, thinly sliced
¼ cup sliced pickled cucumber (see recipe, page 154)
½ cup diced tomatoes
¼ cup sliced green onion
½ teaspoon fresh ginger juice
½ teaspoon sesame oil
2 tablespoons shoyu
1 pinch red chili flakes
1 teaspoon toasted sesame seeds
Sea salt

In a pot of boiling salted water, quickly parboil the warabi. Drain and cool in an ice bath. Drain and set aside. Toss all of the ingredients in a mixing bowl. Season with sea salt.

Serves 4.

This is one of those dishes where Then and Now overlap. My grandma used to make warabi salad with smoked meat, dried shrimp, or kamaboko (fish cake) inside. Then, for years, I kind of lost track of it. I'm not sure why. Maybe it was because people from that older generation started passing away, or because warabi is not easy to find here on O'ahu anymore. Even our vendors have a hard time supplying it. I started playing around with it again at the request of Hukilau co-owner Kurt Osaki, who grew up on Kaua'i. I like the texture as a salad. It has a nice crunch and a little hint of that sap that gives it a "wild" flavor. Now, people are getting back into it again so you'll see it on restaurant menus. You can buy smoked pork and pickled cucumber, or you can use my Kim Chee–Smoked Pork and Pickled Cucumber recipes. -JT

This dish was very popular in the past, especially when aku (katsuo or skipjack tuna) used to be a lot more plentiful than it is now. Today, everything is focused around 'ahi (yellowfin), which has a lighter meat and more subtle flavor than aku. Soaking the aku in a ginger and shoyu marinade helps to kill some of its fishy smell and flavor. The hot rice and hot tea add a comfort factor and turns it into a filling and satisfying meal. This recipe is also great for any kind of sashimi or raw fish you might have left over. –DK

Aku Chazuke

4 tablespoons shoyu
1 tablespoon grated ginger
½ pound aku, 'ahi or other soft-textured fish, cut in 1-inch chunks
2 cups cooked rice
Hot tea (optional)

Mix shoyu and ginger together and marinate fish for at least 30 minutes and up to overnight.

Traditional preparation: This requires freshly made, hot rice. In a deep bowl, spread half the rice and layer marinated fish on top. Layer the remaining rice over the fish. Cover with a plate and let stand for several minutes. Remove cover and stir fish and rice together. Pour hot tea over fish and rice to further cook the fish.

Alternative preparation: In a microwave-safe dish, spread half the rice and layer marinated fish on top. Layer the remaining rice over the fish. Dampen a small kitchen or paper towel and cover rice. Microwave for about a minute (or longer, if you prefer fish completely cooked through). Add hot tea, if you like.

Serves 1.

KAU KAU

'Ahi Katsu Salad with Wasabi–Sesame Dressing

8 ounces sashimi-grade 'ahi, cut into a block (2.5" by 1.5" by 6")
1 half-sheet nori (seaweed)
1 cup flour
1 egg
Ice-cold water

Panko (Japanese bread crumbs)
6 ounces local mixed greens
½ fresh local tomato, sliced
½ avocado, sliced
¼ cup Wasabi–Sesame Dressing (recipe follows)

Wrap 'ahi with nori. Set aside, seam-side down. In a mixing bowl, whisk together the flour and egg. While whisking, add in just enough cold water to make a thin tempura batter—it should be just thick enough to coat your finger. Spread panko on a clean plate. Dip the nori-wrapped 'ahi in the batter and then into the panko, rolling to coat the entire piece. Shake off any excess.

In a deep fryer set at 350°F, quickly flash fry the 'ahi for about 30 seconds or until light golden-brown. Remove from the fryer, blot excess oil on a clean paper towel and immediately slice into ½-inch slices. If you do not cut the fish right away, it will continue to cook.

In a mixing bowl, gently toss greens with dressing. Plate the salad with avocado and tomatoes. Top with 'Ahi Katsu. Extra dressing can also be used as a sauce on top of the 'ahi.

Serves 2.

Wasabi–Sesame Dressing

¼ cup ground toasted sesame seeds
½ cup sugar
¾ cup rice vinegar
3 tablespoons shoyu

3 tablespoons sesame oil
½ cup wasabi powder
½ gallon mayonnaise

In a blender, blend together all of the ingredients except for the mayonnaise. In a mixing bowl combine the contents of the blender with mayonnaise.

Makes ½ gallon.

Poke salad is on the menu almost anywhere you go, so of course we have our own version, too. I'm always trying to experiment, however—different flavors, different ways of adding texture to the dish. In this case, the katsu-style preparation adds crunch on the outside, while leaving the 'ahi raw in the center. It's a very popular dish. Some days it seems like every salad order coming through kitchen is for the 'Ahi Katsu Salad.   -JT

Fried Tofu Soup

This dish was inspired by a visit to Tokkuri Tei, a popular izakaya-style restaurant in Honolulu. I went home and started tinkering on my own using just these very basic ingredients. Fried tofu on its own is outstanding, of course. Its texture is great, and you're simply enhancing the flavor with the dashi (broth) and daikon suri (oroshi, or grated daikon). Instead of using meat, the tofu is the protein, so it's really very healthy and quite economical. Also, when you buy fresh tofu, you often can't eat the whole thing. Instead of wasting it, you can make something—fry it and make delicious soup! -DK

1 teaspoon cooking oil
½ block firm tofu, drained
Cornstarch or flour
1 large or 2 small dried shiitake mushrooms
1 package (.225 ounce) dashi (Japanese soup stock) powder
4 cups warm water
½ cup grated daikon
2 tablespoons grated carrot

Heat oil in a frying pan. Cut tofu into 1½-inch cubes. Coat with cornstarch or flour. Fry until brown on all sides. Remove from pan and rest on paper towels to remove excess oil.

Soak shiitake mushrooms in warm water. When softened, slice into thin strips. Reserve soaking liquid and combine with dashi powder in a soup pot. Add in daikon, carrots and mushrooms. Lower heat once the soup begins to boil and allow it to simmer for about 5 minutes. Place a few cubes of tofu in each individual serving bowl and pour soup to cover.

Serves 4 to 6.

Tofu–Watercress Salad

4 cups watercress, cut into 1-inch lengths
½ cup Watercress Salad Dressing (recipe follows)
1 block tofu, large diced
1 cup tomatoes, diced
½ cup taegu (dried, seasoned cod)
½ cup takuan (pickled radish), julienned
½ cup sliced green onion
1 ounce kaiware (daikon sprouts)
1 tablespoon toasted sesame seeds

In a bowl, toss watercress with dressing. Remove watercress and spread on a serving dish. Gently toss tofu in the same bowl with the remaining dressing and layer on top of watercress. Top with diced tomatoes, followed by taegu, takuan, green onion and kaiware sprouts, each ingredient layered on top the previous. Top with toasted sesame seeds.

Serves 4.

Watercress Salad Dressing

1 cup soybean oil, divided
2½ teaspoons minced garlic
1½ teaspoons minced ginger
½ cup sugar
½ cup shoyu (Yamasa brand preferred)

Slowly cook garlic in ½ cup of oil until almost light golden brown (about 10 minutes). Add ginger and cook until garlic is light golden brown. Add the remaining cup of oil to stop the garlic from overcooking. Set aside to cool. While still warm—but not hot—whisk in remaining ingredients.

Makes 14 ounces.

When I started at the Pagoda, the restaurant had all kinds of items—blocks of tofu, takuan, tomato, watercress, bean sprouts—set out individually on the salad bar. The problem was, nobody was eating them. In order to get people to actually eat salad, I decided to compose a nice one for them. My mom used to make tofu salad with canned tuna and my neighbor used canned salmon, but I couldn't do that in a restaurant. Taegu *(dried, seasoned Korean codfish)* has a different flavor, but retains that seafood element. We have this salad on the banquet menu as well as in the restaurant, all nicely layered and presented. Now, our diners dive into the fresh, healthy salad along with their prime rib, crab and fresh seafood entrées! -JT

I learned this dish from George Yoshida. George and I co-host a cooking show, Seniors Living in Paradise, on Big Island cable television. Every so often, local people will give us pumpkins and this is one of the dishes we like to make with it. It's real old-fashioned food, but it's very good—a great side dish. George insists on using ebi (dried shrimp). I tell him that ebi has gotten too expensive, so I use chicken or pork. George won't ever scrimp, however, and he'll use the best ingredients to get the dish just right. -DK

Kabocha and Ebi
(Pumpkin and Dried Shrimp)

1 medium size kabocha (Japanese pumpkin)
3 teaspoons vegetable oil
10 pieces dried ebi (shrimp)
2 cups water
2 tablespoons shoyu
2 tablespoons sugar
2 aburage (deep fried tofu), optional
6 shiitake mushroom, sliced, optional
Salt

Remove skin, seeds and stringy bits from kabocha and cut into 1½-inch cubes.
Heat oil in a deep saucepan and brown the kabocha and ebi. Add water and bring to
a boil. Do not cover. Allow to simmer until liquid is reduced by half. Mix shoyu
and sugar together and add to pan. Cut aburage, if using, into ½-inch pieces.
Add salt, shiitake and aburage (if using) and continue to simmer uncovered over
medium heat until kabocha is soft.

Serves 4 as an entrée with rice, or 6 to 8 as a side dish.

Roasted Kabocha Risotto

1 kabocha (Japanese pumpkin) or butternut squash
¾ cup uncooked Arborio rice
2 teaspoons vegetable oil
½ cup white wine
8 cups chicken stock (or vegetable stock)
1 cup asparagus
1 cup fresh spinach
½ cup diced tomato
2 tablespoons butter (may be omitted for vegans)
¼ cup shredded Parmesan cheese (may be omitted for vegans)
Olive oil
Salt and pepper

Split squash in half and scoop out the seeds. Lightly rub flesh with olive oil and season with salt and pepper. Place squash on a parchment paper-lined sheet pan, flesh side down. Roast for about 45 minutes at 350°F. To check for doneness, prick the outer skin with a fork or skewer; it should easily penetrate. Use a large spoon to scoop out the flesh; purée in a food processor. Set aside.

Add the raw rice to a sauté pan with vegetable oil. Sauté, constantly moving the pan, being sure to coat each grain of rice with oil. This will give the rice a nutty flavor. Deglaze the pan with white wine. Using a wooden spoon, continue stirring the rice. Once the wine has cooked out, add 1 cup of stock. Season with salt and pepper and continue stirring. When nearly all the stock has been absorbed, add another cup of stock. Continue this process and keep stirring until the rice is almost al dente. This should take about 15 minutes. You may need more stock, or you might not need it all. Every batch is a little different. When the rice is cooked, fold in the asparagus, spinach and 2 cups of roasted kabocha purée. To finish, fold in tomatoes, butter and cheese. Season again with salt and pepper to taste.

Serves 2 to 3.

During my time in California, we used a lot of different types of squashes, such as butternut squash and acorn squash. We roasted them and made dishes like roasted butternut squash ravioli. Back home, my grandma used to always make pork and squash, but the squash wasn't the star of the dish. It took on the flavor of the pork and the shoyu-sugar-ginger sauce. I wanted to do a dish where the squash was the star. By roasting it, the kabocha (Japanese pumpkin) takes on a nice, nutty flavor that makes it the focus of the dish. When I started cooking for my daughter, I always roasted pumpkin or squash, and she loved it. -JT

My dad used to take me to the river to catch ʻōpae. He would hold the net and needed someone to chase the ʻōpae downstream where he waited. When he came looking for a "swampa" (swamper, or assistant) to chase the ʻōpae, my brothers used to run away. Maybe it was because if you went with my dad, you had to work fast. If you moved too slowly, the shrimp would all escape and you'd get scolded. I like my ʻōpae crisp. I don't like it when it's "betabeta" (soggy). Of course, ʻōpae are extremely hard to find these days so if you don't have a source, I guess you're out of luck. (Sorry.) I'm still looking for small shrimp that could substitute for ʻōpae, but all the shrimp farmers want their shrimp to grow big. -DK

Fresh river ʻōpae (small shrimp)
Vegetable oil
Garlic powder
Shoyu
Sugar
Hawaiian chili pepper

Wash ʻōpae thoroughly. Heat oil in a wok over high heat. Add ʻōpae and garlic powder to taste. Stir-fry until the ʻōpae turn red. Add in a mixture of equal parts of shoyu and sugar, and Hawaiian chili pepper to taste. Stir-fry to remove excess liquid. Transfer to an oven-safe pan or a "bowl" made of aluminum foil and crisp in the oven.

Dining on the Wild Side

"Those of us who grew up on the plantation were really lucky," Derek says. "For one thing, we were able to catch all kinds of things from the rivers and the ocean." Hawai'i residents of a certain age will remember when rivers were home to such delicacies as 'ōpae (shrimp), gori ('o'opu or goby fish), crayfish, frogs and wī (hīhī wai or river 'opihi) and ocean-savvy foragers could gather 'a'ama crab, seaweed, wana (sea urchin), namako (sea cucumber) or 'opihi, pipipi, cowry and other edible limpets and mollusks that clung stubbornly to the rocky shore.

Compared to today, Hawai'i's rivers and coastlines were thriving with life, Derek notes. "People knew how to live off of the land. They knew what to eat and how to eat them. Mainly, I think people knew not to take more than they needed." Somewhere along the line, however, highly prized items such as 'opihi became commercially valuable commodities. "You never used to buy 'opihi," Derek recalls. "It was free, but you had to know how to go and get them." Unfortunately, a lot of these resources have been severely depleted in recent times.

In some ways, the term "forage" (to wander around searching) is somewhat of a misnomer. There is nothing accidental or random about foraging. You had to know where to go, when to go and how to go in order to get what you wanted. People employed special baits, techniques and tools. This knowledge was passed down through generations, like recipes, and skillful practitioners were held in high esteem, especially given the dangers posed by life-threatening flash floods, steep cliffs and raging surf that were inevitable factors in all foraging expeditions.

Old-timers knew every nook and corner of the land and even had names for their favorite rivers, ponds and gulches—localized names you're not likely to find on any map. "Get bigger 'ōpae along that flat wall of that pond," Derek's friend and fishing guide, James Ishii, noted on a recent outing. "And there's a hollow in the rock in front of you—should get plenty 'ōpae inside there!"

"It's interesting how some of this knowledge gets passed along," Derek observes. "Take 'opihi. I use the same recipe that came from cooking oysters on the half shell to prepare the 'opihi. Then, on a visit to the Big Island abalone farm, they had to cull out some of the small abalone, so I used that same basic 'opihi recipe on the abalone, too. It turned out delicious." (See page 116 for the 'opihi recipe.)

Live 'ōpae

Crab hunting

Kālua Pig and Shrimp Spring Rolls

1 pound shrimp, chopped into ¼-inch pieces
1 teaspoon sesame oil
1 teaspoon vegetable oil
1 tablespoon finely chopped ginger
½ cup fish sauce
1 dash white pepper
3 cups cabbage, cut into ½-inch pieces
½ cup dried wood ear mushroom, rehydrated and
excess water squeezed out

½ cup shredded carrots
1 cup cellophane noodles, rehydrated and cut into 2-inch
lengths
½ pound kālua pig, shredded
Stir-Fry Sauce (see recipe, page 80)
¼ cup thinly sliced fresh basil
Lumpia wrappers, thawed according to package directions
1 egg yolk
Cooking oil, for frying

In a very hot pan, sauté shrimp in sesame oil and vegetable oil, ginger, fish sauce and white pepper. Set aside to cool.

In a very hot skillet or wok, add vegetables and noodles and sauté briefly. Drain and allow to cool. Fold in cold kālua pig and cooled shrimp. Season with Stir-Fry Sauce (approximately 1 cup). (At this point, any excess lumpia filling can be frozen for future use.) Fold basil gently into the filling mix in batches as you fill and roll the lumpia.

Position a lumpia wrapper with one corner facing directly toward you. Place approximately 2 tablespoons of filling about 2 to 3 inches from the corner nearest you. Fold the corner over so the tip is approximately at the center of the wrapper. Roll filling tightly in wrapper until about half way, then fold the side corners in. Continue rolling away from you and seal the end using egg yolk. (See following pages for step-by-step photo instructions.)

Deep-fry lumpia at 350°F until golden-brown. Do not overcrowd the pan and be careful not to overheat the oil or your wrappers will burn while the filling inside is still cold. Serve with Mandarin Chili Sauce (recipe follows).

Makes filling for 30 to 40 lumpia.

Mandarin Chili Sauce

½ cup shoyu
3 cups sugar
2 cups rice vinegar
1 cup water
¾ cup fish sauce

½ cup sherry
12 cloves garlic, crushed
2 tablespoons crushed red chili flakes
1 tablespoon ginger, crushed
2 cups heavy cream

Combine all ingredients in a sauce pan and simmer for 20 minutes. Strain.

These have been on our menu at the Hukilau from Day One. A lot of spring roll recipes use ground pork. Instead, I wanted a different flavor profile that also added a different texture. The braising/steaming process of cooking kālua pig helps to retain the moisture, giving the spring roll a completely different texture. It adds a smoky element and more depth of flavor. I also liked how it combines Hawaiian and Asian flavors together. -JT

Roll It Up

Lumpia, spring rolls, *temaki*—in Hawai'i we enjoy our wrapped and rolled foods. The preparation of appetizers like these spring rolls is an activity that can be enjoyed by a family or group of friends—and many hands will make the work go faster! Cooks at the Pagoda and Hukilau restaurants often find themselves wrapping hundreds of these for banquet jobs, so Jason's quite the master of the wrap-and-roll technique. A tight wrap and good seal are essential to keep the filling from falling out during the frying stage or when you take a bite.

Position a lumpia wrapper with one corner facing directly toward you and place approximately 2 tablespoons of filling about 2 to 3 inches from the corner nearest you.

Fold the corner over so the tip is approximately at the center of the wrapper.

Roll filling tightly in wrapper away from you until about half way.

Fold the side corners in.

Continue rolling away from you.

Seal the end using egg yolk.

I learned to make kakuma namasu from my sister. The good thing about kakuma (tree fern shoot) is you can boil it and preserve it in water—a process similar to canning. I love kakuma namasu because its flavor is so unique. We usually cook the kakuma with pork or chicken and shoyu-sugar seasoning, but this recipe shares a different style of preparation.

Pickled cabbage, tsukemono, was very important in the plantation days because it was a means of preserving cabbage. It accompanied almost every meal. The process of pickling the cabbage took a period of days, with salt and a heavy stone to slowly press the water out of the cabbage. This recipe is from George Yoshida, who learned it from his mother. It's quick and easy. After you season the cabbage, you just have to refrigerate it for one or two hours and it's ready to eat. No more waiting! –DK

Kakuma Namasu

2 tablespoons dried wakame (seaweed)
2 cups kakuma (hāpu'u, Hawaiian tree
   fern, stalks), sliced
¼ cup shoyu
¼ cup sugar

¼ cup rice vinegar
2 tablespoons shiofuki konbu
   (Japanese dried, salted seaweed)
2 tablespoons dried shrimp
½ cup round onions, sliced

Rehydrate wakame in warm water and slice thinly. Combine all ingredients in a bowl. Mix and refrigerate.

Ingredients Note: See page 128 regarding kakuma. Wakame and shiofuki konbu are different types of seaweed and can be commonly found in most Hawai'i grocery stores or at Japanese or Asian markets. Both come dried, in packages. Shiofuki konbu is seasoned and is usually already shredded, so it does not require rehydration before adding to the other ingredients, as wakame does.

Cabbage Koko

1 4- to 6-inch daikon
1 carrot
½ large or 1 small cabbage, cut into strips
1 cup water
¾ cup sugar
⅓ cup vinegar
2 teaspoons salt

Peel daikon and carrots and cut into ¼-inch thick sticks. Rinse and drain all vegetables. Mix together in a large container.

In a microwave-safe container, combine remaining ingredients. Heat on low power for about 30 to 45 seconds. (Sauce should be warmed just enough to dissolve sugar. Do not overheat.)

Pour sauce over vegetables. Stir and refrigerate overnight. Stir again before serving.

KAU KAU

Kim Chee and Pickled Vegetables

Kim Chee

1 head won bok cabbage
1 cup kosher salt
½ cup Kim Chee Base (recipe follows)
½ cup flat chives, cut into 2-inch lengths

Cut cabbage into 2-inch square pieces, rinse and let drain in a colander. In a mixing bowl, mix salt and cabbage. Toss well. Place a plate (or flat pot lid) directly on the surface of the cabbage. Use a clean, heavy object (canned goods are excellent) to weigh the plate down. Leave at room temperature in a cool area for 8 hours. Rinse well under cold water and let drain in a colander. Gently squeeze out any excess water.

Pour ½ cup of the Kim Chee Base over the cabbage. Mix well and place in a clean container. Cover with an air-tight lid and refrigerate for 24 to 48 hours to let the flavors marry.

Kim Chee Base

1 cup Korean chili flakes
¾ cup fish sauce
1 inch-piece fresh ginger, peeled
3 tablespoons chopped garlic
½ small round onion
½ red bell pepper
1 red jalapeño
2 ounces raw potato, peeled and diced

Combine all of the ingredients in a food processor for 3 to 4 minutes, stopping every minute to scrape down the sides.

Makes enough for 2 to 3 batches of kim chee.

Pickled Vegetables

This is a basic Japanese style pickling brine that you can use for any vegetable. We typically like to use pearl onions, Maui onions, baby radishes, carrots, cucumbers, and hasu (lotus root). Adding red beets to the pickling brine gives color to white vegetables like onions and hasu.

1 cup water
1 cup sugar
1 tablespoon sea salt
1 cup rice vinegar
Red beets (optional)

Heat water, sugar and salt in a saucepan until the sugar and salt is dissolved. Remove from heat and add vinegar. The longer you cook vinegar, the more you will remove that "punch" that you look for in acidity. In this case, we do not want to lose that acidity.

We use kim chee in a lot of our dishes, from fried rice and ramen to sizzling kalbi. I learned a really good recipe from an employee, Sun Cha Han, who was from Korea. In addition to the typical salt, onions, garlic, ginger, fish sauce and chili pepper, an unusual ingredient she incorporated was potato, which added starch and thickened the kim chee sauce a little.

We're familiar with traditional style pickles, like tsukemono and namasu, which look rather plain. In contemporary cuisine, pickles are used to provide visual interest as well as texture and flavor. We use pickled hasu chips, for example, or beets, which add a nice magenta color for presentation purposes along with adding crunch. It both brightens up the dish and balances the flavors out. -JT

This is something new that we created out of something old. We've always had access to a good supply of grass-fed beef here on the Big Island, and we make our own Mountain Apple Brand® pipi kaula at KTA in partnership with our supplier, Kulana Foods. Smoking the meat to make pipi kaula also allows us to use some of the cuts that are harder to sell. We were looking for ways to better utilize and market our product, and making poke with the pipi kaula has proven to be a huge hit. Not everybody likes fish, so by putting Pipi Kaula Poke in the poke case, all of a sudden we're selling 10 times more pipi kaula than we ever did before. It's the perfect pūpū with beer, or you can even eat it with rice as a meal! -DK

Pipi Kaula Poke

2 pounds pipi kaula, sliced
3 to 4 tablespoons sesame oil
½ cup ogo (seaweed), chopped
¼ cup sliced Maui onions
1 tablespoon Hawaiian salt
½ tablespoon dried chilli pepper
2 tablespoons 'inamona (roasted kuku'i nut), optional
Green onions, chopped (for garnish)

Combine all ingredients in a bowl. Chill before serving.

Smoked Shutome Belly

3 pounds shutome (swordfish) belly
1½ cups shoyu
1 cup sugar
½ cup water
3 cloves garlic, crushed
1 2-inch piece of ginger, sliced
Pinch crushed red pepper flakes

Cut the fish into 2-inch by 2-inch by 6-inch blocks. Combine all remaining ingredients for the marinade. Place fish in a plastic zip-top bag and pour marinade over. Seal bag tightly and lay in a container (just in case it leaks). Marinate overnight, turning the bag every 4 hours. (You can take a break to sleep!)

Preheat smoker to 180°F and smoke with kiawe wood for 2 hours. Slice into ¼-inch pieces and serve on a bed of cabbage for a pūpū, or with rice as an entrée.

When you buy shutome *(swordfish)*, you buy it for the steaks, the nice loin cuts, which have a firm texture. The belly portion is very oily. If you try to cook it like you would other fish, it turns out junk. You won't get any of the flakiness. Some things need to be tweaked, and this is definitely one you have to know how to prepare properly. That may be one reason why you don't find shutome belly in the supermarket. Bring in my favorite smoker! Smoked marlin steaks can get kind of dry, but marinate the belly portion for about two days, smoke it low-and-slow, and that thing will turn out amazing—the texture of butterfish. It will melt in your mouth. *-JT*

The first thing that comes to mind when I think of this dish is: "Old Faithful!" Every plantation home had Vienna sausage in its pantry. If you didn't have anything else to eat, you could just pop open a can of Vienna sausage and eat it right out of the can with rice. It was the "go-to" food whenever you were feeling tired and didn't want to cook. When you take the time to make Vienna sausage with shoyu and sugar… Man, you just took it up five notches. It elevates it to "gourmet" status! I still like to eat it today from time to time as a special treat. As a bonus, it's interesting that the price of Vienna sausage is still very affordable, while the cost of other food items has gone up a lot more. -DK

Vienna Sausage Shoyu-Style

1 4.6-ounce can Vienna sausage
1 teaspoon sugar
1 tablespoon shoyu

Empty contents of can (including the liquid) into a frying pan. When sausage is heated, add sugar and shoyu. Remove from heat and roll sausages in pan to coat in sauce. Serve over rice or as a breakfast side.

Serves 1 as an entrée.

Pastrami Reuben Sandwich

Brined Beef Brisket (see recipe, page 72)
⅓ cup cracked black pepper
⅓ cup crushed juniper berries
¼ cup cracked coriander

Mix seasonings together and rub onto brisket. Let sit overnight. Smoke at 200°F for 4 hours. Transfer to oven and continue to cook in a foil-covered pan at 275°F for an additional 4 hours. Let rest for 20 minutes before slicing into ⅛-inch thick pieces. Serve with Swiss cheese, sauerkraut and Russian dressing on marbled rye bread.

For our honeymoon, my wife and I went to New York City. One of our priorities, of course, was going out to eat. New York is known for its delis, so we had to eat the famous pastrami. Since my hobby is smoking meats, I knew right away that I had to try and make my own pastrami back home. The Big Island grass-fed brisket is brined for 10 days. Then, some of it becomes corned beef (see page 72). The meat that becomes pastrami is smoked for four hours and cooked for four more. It takes 10-and-a-half to 11 days to finish the final product. -JT

Smoking 101

Jason's passion for smoking meats developed during the time he spent in California. "Here in Hawai'i, 'barbecue' means grilling something soaked in teriyaki sauce. On the Mainland, barbecue was a whole different world, involving pork shoulders, briskets, ribs and more," he explains. When he began experimenting with smoking items for the Pagoda, he brought his personal smoker from home to work. "A lot of the dishes I do now came about because my smoker at home is kind of big. It's a traditional charcoal smoker, too, so, when you're going to fire it up, you don't want to smoke just one or two pieces. You fill up the whole smoker with whatever you have to experiment with."

The whole process to make pastrami takes 10 to 11 days. It starts with Brined Beef Brisket (see page 72), which is smoked for four hours and then finished in the oven at low temperature for another four hours.

A spice rub transforms the brisket from corned beef into pastrami.

Wood chips are soaked prior to adding them to the smoker.

The smoker is loaded with wood chips.

Brined beef brisket is covered with a rub of spices.

The spice rub-covered brisket is transferred to the smoker.

After smoking for four hours, the brisket cooks in an oven for four more hours.

This is a winner. You can try substituting different kinds of luncheon meat, but somehow Hawai'i folks can always tell the true SPAM® products from everything else. Although the ingredients are basically the same, SPAM® products fry up nice and crispy with just the right texture and taste. But you can substitute foods like tonkatsu or teriyaki meat as the musubi filling, instead of SPAM® products. The combination of teri beef and kim chee is a winner. There's no limit, really. Just use your imagination. -DK

1 can of SPAM® product, any variety(save the can)
Furikake (seasoned seaweed flakes), optional
4 nori (seaweed) sheets, halved
Cooked Calrose (medium-grain) rice

Cut the SPAM® block into 8 slices (the slices should fit perfectly back into the can). Fry the SPAM® slices until brown and crisp on the outside. (Avoid overcooking, as this will make the SPAM® slices rubbery.)

In the SPAM® brand can, add a ½-inch thick layer of rice. Pack rice down with a spoon. Sprinkle furikake (about ½ teaspoon) over the rice. Layer a SPAM® slice over the furikake, topped by another layer of rice. The SPAM® slices and rice layers should not reach higher than halfway up the can. Pack down firmly with a spoon. Invert the can over a half-sheet of nori (it should fit exactly); the stack of SPAM® slices, rice and furikake should slide right out. Tightly wrap the musubi with the nori. Wet the blade of a knife and slice into 3 pieces. (See following pages for step-by-step photo instructions.)

Makes 8 whole musubi or 24 pieces.

SPAM® Musubi...Can!

What sets this version of SPAM® musubi apart is that Derek makes it in an empty SPAM® brand can. "This is important," he says, "because I want everyone to know that no matter where you are in the world, if you have a SPAM® brand can, you can make musubi. You don't need a special press. Save the can! Clean it out and make it one of the implements in your kitchen along with your knives and things." It certainly is an easy way to make musubi when you're camping or traveling away from home and hungry for a taste of Hawai'i.

Pack cooked rice in the bottom of an empty SPAM® brand can.

Sprinkle furikake over the rice.

Layer a SPAM® slice over the furikake.

Top with another layer of rice.

Invert the can; the stack of SPAM® slice, rice and furikake should slide right out.

Tightly wrap the musubi with nori.

Slice into 3 pieces.

Smoked Pork Belly Bahn Mi Sandwich

1 crusty hoagie roll
4 ounces Smoked Pork Belly (recipe follows), rough
   chopped
¼ cup Pickled Carrots and Daikon (recipe follows)

1 teaspoon rough chopped cilantro leaves
1 teaspoons rough chopped mint leaves
1 tablespoon Cilantro–Mint Aioli (recipe follows)

Spread Cilantro–Mint Aioli inside the hoagie roll. Layer pork belly, pickled vegetables and herbs in the roll.

Serves 1.

Smoked Pork Belly

2 pounds pork belly
1½ cup shoyu
1 cup brown sugar
½ cup water

1 piece star anise
1 2-inch piece of ginger, crushed
2 cloves garlic, crushed

Combine all ingredients together and marinate pork belly for 24 hours. Remove pork
from marinade and smoke with apple wood or kiawe wood for 4 hours.

Pickled Carrots and Daikon

½ cup julienned carrots
½ cup julienned daikon
1cup sugar

1 cup rice vinegar
1 cup water
2 teaspoon salt

Mix all ingredients together and allow to sit for at least 4 hours, preferably overnight. Makes 1 cup.

Cilantro–Mint Aioli

1 cup mayonnaise
1 garlic clove, finely minced
½ teaspoon sriracha

1 tablespoon chopped cilantro
1 tablespoon chopped mint

Purée all ingredients in a blender. Makes 1 cup.

I'm a big fan of Vietnamese food, especially pho. "Bahn mi" refers to the type of Vietnamese bread—a crusty baguette—that is used to make Vietnamese bahn mi sandwiches. We use a hoagie roll that is nice and soft in the middle. When we receive an order, we bake the roll whole to crust the outside a little bit. This is kind of a fusion treatment, with the smoked pork belly paired with pickled daikon and carrots, and a nice cilantro–mint aioli. It's very popular as a soup and sandwich special. -JT

Natto (fermented soybeans) is the kind of food that you either love or hate. I happen to think natto is fantastic! When we were young, we used to mix natto with a raw egg and serve it over hot rice— garnish it with green onions, pour some shoyu on top and dive in. Due to food-safety concerns, most people steer clear of raw egg dishes, so that's why I came up with this cooked version. I saw a variety of natto dishes in Japan, including natto sushi. That led me to think, "Why not natto fried rice?" Cooking the natto with eggs and rice turns it into a completely different dish and actually makes it a lot more palatable. It's not stringy or smelly—at least, I don't think so!—and the whole thing has a nice, nutty flavor. Even people who don't normally like natto will enjoy it this way. -DK

Natto Fried Rice

1 package natto (fermented soybeans; see Note)
1 teaspoon shoyu
1 egg
2 teaspoons vegetable oil
¼ cup diced round onions
¼ cup diced string beans (optional)
2 cups cooked rice
1 teaspoon garlic powder
2 teaspoons sesame oil
2 stalks green onion, diced

Combine natto with mustard, shoyu and egg. Mix thoroughly (it will be very stringy). Heat 1 teaspoon of vegetable oil in a frying pan. Briefly fry natto mixture for about 1 to 2 minutes. Remove from pan and set aside. In the same frying pan, heat 1 teaspoon of vegetable oil and fry round onions and string beans briefly before adding rice and garlic powder. Add natto mixture to the rice and fold in. When natto has been evenly distributed, add sesame oil and green onions. Continue to mix fried rice throughout the process to avoid burning. Serve when completely heated through.

Serves 1 to 2.

Note: Natto can be purchased at Asian food grocers, and commonly in supermarkets in Hawai'i. Most brands include a packet of sauce and a packet of hot mustard. For this recipe, be sure to purchase a brand that includes a mustard packet.

Kālua Pig Hash Benedict with Lomi Tomato

1 English muffin, split in half
2 3-ounce portions Kālua Pig Hash (recipe follows)
    formed into patties
2 eggs, soft-poached

2 tablespoons of Hollandaise Sauce (recipe follows)
2 teaspoons Lomi Tomato (recipe follows)
Vegetable oil

Toast the English muffin and set aside. Heat 1 teaspoon of vegetable oil in a nonstick pan over medium-high heat. Cook Kālua Pig Hash patties for 2 minutes on each side, or until golden brown. Place one patty on each English muffin slice. Top each with a soft-poached egg. Lace each egg with one tablespoon of Hollandaise Sauce and top with a teaspoon of Lomi Tomato.

Serves 1.

Kālua Pig Hash

2 pounds kālua pig
1½ pounds frozen shredded hash brown potatoes (not patties)
1 egg

½ cup sliced green onion
Salt and pepper

Combine all ingredients and season with salt and pepper to taste.

Hollandaise Sauce

2 egg yolks
1 teaspoon white wine
1 teaspoon fresh lemon juice
¼ cup warm clarified butter
1 dash of hot sauce
Salt

Bring a small pot of water to a simmer. Add egg yolks, lemon juice and white wine to a stainless steel mixing bowl. Place bowl over the simmering pot and whisk vigorously. As the egg mixture begins to thicken, remove from heat. This change will happen very quickly; remove the eggs immediately to avoid ending up with scrambled eggs. Away from the heat, slowly add clarified butter to the egg mixture a few drops at a time, while whisking vigorously. This emulsifying step is very important. If you add the butter too fast, it will separate and you will have to start all over again. After all the butter is incorporated, add a dash of hot sauce and season with salt. You may also add more lemon juice to your liking.

I'm confident this is a good dish because the servers all recommend it to their customers. And the reason they do that is because they consistently receive good feedback from other customers on it. The kālua pork provides a nice local twist to a breakfast classic, and the lomi tomatoes add a nice pop of color and bright flavor to the dish. -JT

Lomi Tomato

1½ teaspoons finely diced Roma tomato
1 teaspoon finely diced Maui onion
½ teaspoon finely sliced green onion
Pinch of Hawaiian sea salt
Dash of rayu oil (sesame chili oil)

Mix together well.

Arnold Hiura and his late father, Toshika, pounding mochi at their home in Pāpaʻikou, December 1997.

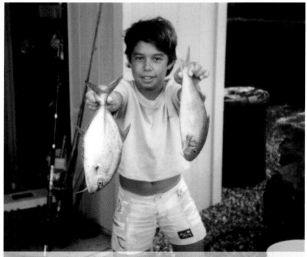

An 11-year-old Jason Takemura shows off his fishing catch

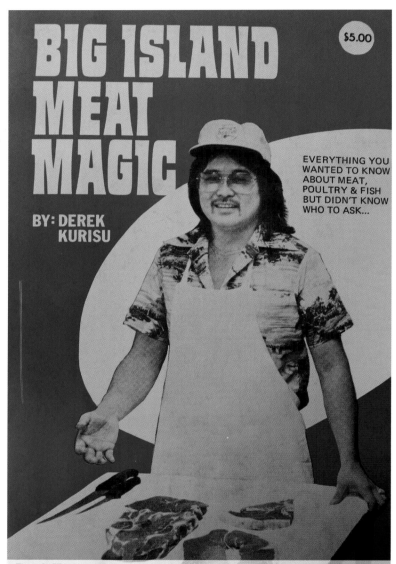

Derek Kurisu on the cover of a KTA meat and fish preparation booklet from the late 1970s.

Epilogue: Staying Connected

Discussions of Hawai'i's local cuisine can become confusing, especially to the uninitiated. There is, on the one hand, a familiar list of local favorites such as beef stew, loco moco, chili and rice, saimin, SPAM® musubi and plate lunches. These popular dishes—often fast, tasty, cheap and filling—are commonly served at hole-in-the-wall diners, drive-ins and venerable, old-style lunch wagons.

Then, one might look online or pick up a travel or lifestyle magazine touting Hawai'i's contemporary food scene, led by internationally renowned HRC chefs and a new generation of rising stars who are putting their own unique stamp on the culinary landscape. This category of cuisine—innovative, imaginative and elegantly presented—is associated with high-end restaurants and hip, new dining establishments.

What is usually ignored is a third category of food—the kind that has always existed under the radar, unaffected by the shifting tides of fashion and popularity. This is the food that local people have eaten in the privacy of their homes for decades—food that they caught, hunted, raised, shared or gathered themselves from the sea, the rivers, the forests and the farms of Hawai'i. These dishes—fresh, local and natural—are sometimes unnamed and not available in any restaurant.

More and more, however, the chasm between the simple, the fancy and the homemade is being bridged. Food trucks and unpretentious restaurants serve high-end food at a moderate cost. Elite restaurants are turning out haute cuisine versions of common local food, raw fish, shellfish and foraged greens.

Today, simple homespun fare is enjoying a renewed level of respect and appreciation. By maintaining a relationship with the past, what we eat helps to define who we are. By extension, if we disconnect ourselves from the past, we will be alienated from the culture that forms the foundation of our most basic social behaviors and beliefs. Food, after all, has always served as a bridge that joins people.

In a time long before cell phones, parents' voices were the dinner bells that echoed across Hawai'i's urban and rural landscapes. "Kau kau time!" those voices would call, beckoning kids determined to squeeze the last few ounces of sunlight out of the quickly descending dusk.

In the old folk tale, Hansel and Gretel left a trail of breadcrumbs through the forest so the way home would not be lost. Greedy birds gobbled up all the bread, leaving the children hopeless, alone and hungry. There's a lesson there for us today: to take better care of our own precious morsels from the past, so that we can always find our own way home!

Derek Kurisu: The "Then" Master

Derek Kurisu is executive vice president of KTA Super Stores, a locally owned supermarket with six stores on the Big Island of Hawai'i. While his official title may sound familiar in today's corporate world, trying to explain what Derek actually does defies description. His days are a dizzying maze of activity that could take him from nameless country roads to the boardrooms of Hawai'i's most influential decision makers, from preparing lunch for residents at a long-term care home to emceeing a massive, sold-out event at one of Waikīkī's glitzy banquet halls—sometimes all in the same day.

On paper, at least, Derek's primary responsibility at KTA is to oversee purchasing, particularly for its perishable food operations. Far from playing a traditional "behind-the-scenes" management role, however, Derek is one of the most widely recognized personalities in Hawai'i. Known for his booming voice, inexhaustible sense of humor and self-deprecating, country boy style, it's not hard to see why Derek's popularity encompasses people of all ages, ethnicities and economic backgrounds.

Derek's public persona is driven in part by two local cable television programs that he produces. He serves as the on-air host for *Living in Paradise* and co-host, with George Yoshida, on *Seniors Living in Paradise*. Both shows change monthly, but are aired twice daily for an entire month. In addition to promoting products available at KTA, each show contains cooking segments and features noteworthy community events and individuals.

Derek started working for KTA as a "bag boy" while still in high school. Bag boys not only packed groceries, but assisted customers in loading their cars. "I remember that to get the job you had to show them you could carry a 100-pound bag of rice," he said. With the encouragement and support of Tony Taniguchi, then president of KTA, Derek attended the University of Hawai'i at Mānoa, where he earned a degree in agriculture and quickly returned to the Big Island to work at KTA.

It was in the early '80s that Tony took Derek aside and asked him what he would do to help people when the sugar industry closed. "I didn't know what to say," Derek recalls. "At the time, you couldn't even conceive of plantations closing. It seemed that sugar would go on forever." Tony proved to be prophetic, however, and had the incredible foresight to arm his young staff to plan for the future. "When the sugar plantations go under, everyone is going to come to you," he warned Derek, "and you've got to be able to help the people."

Although he couldn't quite grasp all of what his boss was talking about at the time, Derek soon came to grips with it and came up with what is already an inspired Hawai'i food tradition in its own right: Mountain Apple Brand® products. Sadly, Tony died in 1989 at the age of 59 and was not able to see for himself the results of his guidance and the outcomes of the challenges he presented to Derek.

Derek launched Mountain Apple Brand® as KTA's private label in 1992. Driven by his desire to help displaced plantation workers, Derek worked directly with vendors, including some with one-of-a-kind recipes, to help them through the challenges of starting a business and producing their products commercially. "Small vendors put their whole heart into a product," Derek says. "We help them by packaging, distributing and marketing their products for them under the Mountain Apple label."

Even with seasonal fluctuations, today there are more than 240 items sold under the Mountain Apple label, supplied by some 60-plus local vendors. Products range from fresh milk and eggs, to grass-fed beef and Island lamb. There are freshly baked breads and cookies, local coffee and unique desserts. Mountain Apple also offers a wide range of locally grown fruits and fresh vegetables, including an assortment of pre-packaged salads and vacuum-packed vegetables. Mountain Apple is also known for its traditional ethnic foods, such as dried and smoked fish, sushi, poi, boiled peanuts, pickled vegetables and seaweed. Derek estimates that 90 percent of KTA's leafy vegetables are locally produced; 30 to 40 percent of the beef sold is raised on the Big Island; 100 percent of papayas and bananas are local, as is every drop of fresh milk sold at KTA. All of this lends a farmers market ambiance to KTA's operations.

Mountain Apple offers a significant kick-start for anyone seeking to launch a new product. Derek's goal is for each entrepreneur to eventually be successful enough to expand to their own label and distribution outside of KTA. Indeed, his advocacy of local products far exceeds the confines of KTA stores.

Derek's far-reaching efforts earned him the SBA Minority Small Business Advocate of the Year award in 1997 and the University of Hawai'i College of Tropical Agriculture and Human Resources (CTAHR) Alumnus of the Year recognition in 2002. He has also taken leadership roles in such statewide organizations as the Hawai'i Food Industry Association (HFIA), serving as its chair in 2006, and as co-chair of the state Agribusiness Development Corporation.

Derek also chairs "Hoku," an organization he was instrumental in forming, informally comprised of groups working to establish a collaboration between public and private sector entities, including: HFIA, Hawai'i Food Manufacturers Association, Department of Agriculture, CTAHR, Hawai'i Farm Bureau Federation, Hawai'i Restaurant Association, Chamber of Commerce of Hawai'i, Hawai'i Marketing Alliance, Mānoa Innovation Center and the Career and Technical Education Department–U.S. Department of Education. It is, to say the least, an impressive representation of movers and shakers that Derek has managed to gather at the same table with the shared goal of making the state's food supply safer and more sustainable, as well as helping the economy.

KTA will observe its centennial anniversary in 2016, and Derek recognizes that while it is important to keep up the fight to promote local products and agriculture in Hawai'i, there is a lot more on the line. To understand his deeper mission, one has to go back to Derek's roots growing up in the sugar plantation town of Hakalau, about 12 miles north of Hilo along the Hāmākua Coast. It was there that he first discovered his affinity with food. "I always liked to cook," he recalls. "I cooked so often that my father would tease me for doing 'women's work,' but I never listened to him. He would get it from my mother, too."

In his heart, Derek's broader mission is to preserve the values of Aloha that were instilled in him during his plantation days—food is one of the tools he uses to share his message with others. "When I speak to students, I always bring up how we lived on the plantation, because they need to know those values," he says. "People valued humility and honesty; they respected each other and shared what they had. Those are things worth keeping, don't you think?"

Chef Jason Takemura:
Serving Tradition with Innovation

Two miles of busy city streets separate the Hukilau Restaurant in downtown Honolulu and the Pagoda Floating Restaurant near Ala Moana Shopping Center. As executive chef for both venues, it's a distance that Chef Jason Takemura knows intimately. The two restaurants provide a fascinating culinary contrast, with the Hukilau catering almost exclusively to a downtown business crowd, while the Pagoda has long been the favorite of an older, more traditional clientele.

Meeting the expectations of these two disparate audiences serves to remind Jason on a daily basis that a chef has to be constantly mindful of whom he is cooking for. It is a mantra that Jason has maintained throughout his entire professional life.

After completing his studies at the Western Culinary Institute (Le Cordon Bleu College of Culinary Arts) in Portland, Oregon, Jason headed south along the West Coast to hone his skills at several of California's best-known restaurants, including Roy's at Pebble Beach, Montrio Bistro in Monterey, Seven Hands on Higuera in San Luis Obispo and the Inn at Spanish Bay, Pebble Beach Resorts.

Jason was just 25 years old when he returned to Hawai'i to work for Chef Chai Chaowasaree at the popular Chai's Island Bistro and quickly worked his way up to executive chef. While there, Jason eagerly tried to incorporate some of his Mainland-inspired concepts into Chai's Asian/Pacific-Rim menu, only to be met with an underwhelming reception. "It was a rude awakening," he admits frankly.

Not only were his specials not moving, but Jason began to feel as though he had stepped into a time warp, with diners here lagging far behind the trends already established on the Mainland. "I tried to do more California-style cuisine and introduce different ingredients, like stuffed quail, wild mushrooms, *foie gras*," Jason explains, "but things that sold like crazy on the Mainland, people here wouldn't even order."

Jason immediately began adjusting his dishes, emphasizing their local and Asian profiles. He incorporated more familiar flavors, locally grown ingredients, and tweaked the consistency of dishes like risotto so that rice-loving locals enjoyed it more. "I learned a lot from working with Chai, especially about balancing flavors and textures," Jason says. "I also worked on getting the wait staff on board, so that they could communicate better with the customers. In the end, people liked what we were doing," he reports.

In 2007, after four years at Chai's, Jason was chosen to open the new Hukilau restaurant in downtown Honolulu as its executive chef. Then, four years later, his responsibilities grew to encompass the food service operations at the Pagoda Hotel & Floating Restaurant as well.

Overseeing both restaurants marked quite a milestone in Jason's culinary journey, the start of which began in 1998 as a part-time employee at Pietro's. "I loved it," he recalls. After Pietro's, Jason went to work at Suntory Restaurant, where he learned about upscale Japanese food—including sushi and teppanyaki—from Suntory's executive chef from Japan. "This is what I want to do," Jason boldly informed his parents, then left the University of Hawai'i at Mānoa to enroll at the Western Culinary Institute (Le Cordon Bleu College of Culinary Arts) in Portland.

"If you're lucky, you had parents and grandparents who cooked," Jason observes. "These days, people hardly cook, and kids aren't exposed to traditional foods. At my house, my mom cooked weekdays and Dad cooked on the weekends. Maybe that's why I always liked to cook from when I was very young."

While attending high school at Mid-Pacific Institute, Jason moved in with his grandparents. "They had a two-story house, so I cleaned out the downstairs storage space and furnished it. It had a separate entrance, so it made for a perfect bachelor's pad." Jason shared the kitchen with his grandmother, however, and ate his meals with them, so there was lots of traditional local food on his plate.

"My grandparents definitely made a big impact on who I am today—how they treated people, their generosity," Jason recalls. "They had a big mango tree in the yard, and when the tree had mangoes, Grandpa would pick them so Grandma could make mango muffins to give to the neighbors."

Both of Jason's grandparents are gone now, but he remains very much connected to them, as he now lives in their house with his wife, Jana, daughter, Saige, and newborn son, Tanner.

"A lot of the younger parents today don't cook at home," Jason observes. "Both parents work, so they eat out a lot. That culture of traditional family meals is fast disappearing." In his case, as if running one restaurant wasn't tough enough, Jason has to oversee two, including a busy weekend banquet schedule at the Pagoda.

In spite of the challenges, Jason takes pride in becoming his daughter's private chef. "Her first table food was boiled edamame, puréed with breast milk," he says proudly. Now two years old, Saige loves going to the supermarket and the farmers market with her parents. "She knows a lot," Jason beams. "She smells all the fruits. She knows their names. She's all into it." Having a child has profoundly affected how Jason cooks at home, he explains. "I cook a lot lighter and healthier—more veggies, more trips to the farmers market—and not as much fatty food."

Food is all about making connections, Jason concludes. "Food connects people; it connects past and present; it keeps us connected to our values." Soon after moving into his grandparents' house, Jason discovered the family's old *mochi* machine in a downstairs storage area. "I dug it out and took it to my mom's house," he reports. "That year, we revived the family mochi-making tradition together with my brother and his kids. We're very lucky to have that connection."

Jason also notes that most of his neighbors are original area residents, contemporaries of his grandparents. "They're in their 80s or 90s now," he says, "so it's not like we have a lot in common with them. However, when one of them saw that I was [working] at the Pagoda, he went to pick up the other neighbors and they all came to eat at the restaurant. That felt really good, for them to show their support like that!" It's just the sort of experience that helps to keep Jason grounded, and a reminder that, then and now, food has a special savor when we're fed by someone we know.

The Pagoda opened in 1964, well over a decade before Jason was even born. Not long after starting his tenure there, Jason began spearheading an effort to revive and transform the restaurant facilities. After a few delays, renovations are now underway. "Our plan is to preserve the character and feel of the place while upgrading and modernizing other features," he explains. "We'll remove some things that just don't make sense but have simply been left as-is for years."

Keeping the special things from the past and making improvements for the future, adapting our heritage for the modern day—exactly the direction Jason and his generation of younger chefs are taking our local food.

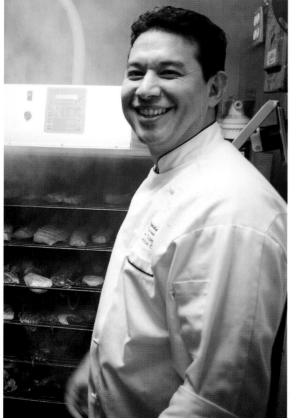

Arnold's Acknowledgments

Book Partners: Eloise Hiura, Derek Kurisu, Jason Takemura, Kurt Osaki, Duane Kurisu, George Engebretson and Dawn Sakamoto.

Family for love and support: Satomi Hiura, Andrea Hiura, Alyssa Hiura, Joey & Randene Itagaki, Raina Itagaki, Tiffany Kim & Taylor. Karen Konishi, Kyle & Susan Kanetake, Brett & Lauri Yamashita, Kevin Konishi, Milton Hiura & Carol Kato. Garret Horiuchi, Jessica Horiuchi, Tom Flores, Mom Ruby, Randy & Joan Okumura, John & Hilma Fujimoto, Lloyd & Susan Nakama, Terron & Dee Oshiro, Tyson Oshiro and Tag.

Very supportive friends: Allan & Irma Ikawa, Sherrie Ann Holi, Lance Duyao, Barry & Sandy Taniguchi, Glenn Yamanoha, Stephan & Saori Doi, Russell & René Tomita, Lesli Marumoto, Shuzo Uemoto, Bob Nakamura & Karen Ishizuka, Tad Nakamura, Daryl Higashi & Linda Ueda, Mike Tomihara & Sandy Mar, Alan & Sharlene Miyamura, Rosie Tatsuguchi & Tom Shizuru and James Ishii.

Special shout-out to *Kau Kau* lovers in San Francisco and San Jose!

Derek's Acknowledgments

I wish to thank:

My wife, Georganne, and son, Blake, for being my inspiration and providing the support and guidance in whatever I undertake.

My grandparents, parents and in-laws for your sacrifices, lessons and teaching me those sugar plantation values.

My Aunty Doris Ito and my late Uncle Sonny for being my second set of parents. Special thanks to Aunty Kay Yonemori who is always there for our family and my brothers-in-law, Bill Kaono and Jimmy Ishii, on whom I depend for everything!

Members of the Kurisu and Murai families for always being there for me.

The owners of KTA for providing me with the opportunities to do what I love and believe in.

All of the employees, business partners and associates of KTA for your hard work and support to make everything possible.

To my friends and their families, all those memorable eating and party experiences were lessons on food and fun and will be with me forever.

George and Cheryl Yoshida for teaching and helping me.

The seniors who inspire me and the youth who motivate me to always try to do the right thing.

Jason's Acknowledgments

I'd like to personally thank my beautiful family Jana, Saige and Tanner Takemura, for being my inspiration. You continue to sacrifice and support me and my dreams and put up with the long hours of being a chef. Without you, this wouldn't have been possible. I love you!

Thank you to my parents for believing in me and allowing me to be on this path.

Thank you to my brother, Alex Takemura, for always beating me in Nintendo while we were growing up. We always played so that the loser would have to cook for the winner. In the end, even if I won, I would still end up cooking because I had developed the love of cooking, and because mine always tasted better!

Thank you to my two grandmothers, Madelyn Levenson (Bubbie) and the late Sumiko Takemura. I was lucky enough to grow up watching you cook in the kitchen and learning the meaning of family. This is where I first learned how satisfying it was to cook for others and to put your heart and soul into every dish. You both truly inspire me to be the best I can be.

Thank you to the late Kengo Takemura (grandfather) for showing me the meaning of the word "sacrifice" and your great work ethic to provide for your family.

Thank you to my business partners, Duane Kurisu, Kurt Osaki and Rodney Park, for giving me this great opportunity to follow my dreams in being a restaurant owner. Though we started as business partners, I am very proud to also call you my friends.

Thank you to my Hukilau and Pagoda family for all of the support and hard work. Without all of you, none of this would have been possible.

Thank you to Derek Kurisu and Arnold Hiura for your hard work and for sharing all of your stories and knowledge.

Thank you to Dawn Sakamoto and Rae Huo for all of your hard work and patience during the photo shoots.

Thank you to Chef Chai Chaowasaree. I've learned so much from working with you in the kitchen. You are a great friend and inspiration to me.

Glossary
A guide to ingredients.

ʻAhi Hawaiian name for yellowfin tuna ("maguro" in Japanese), great grilled or as sashimi or poke.

Aku Hawaiian name for skipjack tuna ("katsuo" in Japanese); can be eaten as poke or sashimi, but is usually fried, or salted and dried.

ʻAʻama Crab Thin-shelled Hawaiian rock crab, salted and eaten raw.

Bonito A type of tuna, similar to aku, used to make katsuobushi.

Black Beans Referring to Chinese salted and fermented black beans, either in dried form, or bottled with other ingredients in a paste-like form.

Chinese Parsley The local term for cilantro. So commonly used, it often appears on grocery store signs, rather than "cilantro." (This book uses the terms interchangeably.)

Daikon Japanese term for white radish. It has a mild flavor and shows up in soups or one-pot dishes as well as grated (often paired with shoyu) in dipping sauces or as a garnish. They are common in Vietnamese cuisine, pickled and shredded.

Dashi Japanese word for cooking stock, used to make broths and soups. Some cooks make their own with konbu and katsuobushi but powdered dashi base is readily found in markets.

Ebi Dried shrimp used in many Asian dishes. Sold in packages, they can be eaten whole.

Fish Sauce In Hawaiʻi, the Filipino variant ("patis") is the default, but it is also the flavor base for many Southeast Asian dishes. It has a very pungent characteristic smell.

Furikake Japanese seasoning made of dried seaweed, salt, sesame seeds and bonito flakes.

Gyoza Wrappers Also called potsticker, won ton or dumpling wrappers. Circular in shape and found in Asian markets. (In Hawaiʻi grocery stores, they're usually found with the tofu and fresh, uncooked noodles.)

ʻInamona Kukui (candlenut tree) nut meat, roasted, grated and mixed with salt to season a variety of Hawaiian dishes—especially poke.

Kabocha Japanese pumpkin; it has dark green skin and bright orange flesh. Kabocha are small and hard, often with bumpy skin.

Kakuma Japanese term for Hawaiian tree fern ("hāpuʻu") stalks.

Kālua Pig Hawaiian roast pig, traditionally baked in an imu.

Kamaboko Japanese fish cake.

Kampachi Yellowtail amberjack or kahala fish. Kampachi is farmed on the Big Island and sold under the name Hawaiian Kampachi™.

Katsuobushi Dried, fermented and smoked bonito or skipjack tuna. Once dried, it is shaved paper-thin and used as the basis for dashi (broth) or used as a garnish on dishes to add an umami quality. (This book uses the term "bonito flakes" interchangeably.)

Kim Chee Korean dish of pickled and fermented vegetables, often seasoned with chili peppers

Ko Choo Jang Korean chili pepper sauce.

Konbu (or Kombu) Japanese term for kelp ("dashima" in Korean or "haidai" in Chinese); most commonly sold in dried strips or sheets. Used to make broth ("dashi") and sometimes as an ingredient in one-pot dishes. When rehydrated, it is thick and rubbery or leather-like in texture.

Lumpia Wrappers Also called spring roll wrappers. (Lumpia are the Filipino version of spring rolls.) Larger and thinner than gyoza wrappers—these wrappers are tissue paper-thin—and square, rather than round. These are usually sold frozen and must be thawed before use.

Mirin Japanese rice wine used for cooking. Sweeter and with lower alcohol content than sake.

Miso Thick, fermented paste made of rice, barley and/or soybeans, used in Japanese cooking. White ("shiro") and red ("aka") are most commonly seen.

Natto Japanese fermented soybean dish.

Nori Thin dried sheets of seaweed used in Japanese cooking as a garnish or to make sushi or musubi.

Ogo Japanese term for a type of seaweed ("limu" in Hawaiian). Ogo can refer to many types of seaweed, but they are characteristically moss-like in appearance (as opposed to the kelp sheets or konbu or wakame). Often used for flavoring in poke dishes.

ʻŌpae Hawaiian term for shrimp; the small (less than 2 inches long) river ʻōpae have become rare and are a great treat at local parties.

ʻOpihi Hawaiian term for limpet, usually eaten raw (with salt).

Pipi Kaula Hawaiian dried, spiced beef, similar to beef jerky. Literally, "rope beef."

Poke Hawaiian dish made with cubed raw fish and various ingredients such as onions, limu, Hawaiian salt, shoyu, red chili peppers, sugar and ʻinamona.

Sambal Oelek Indonesian garlic chili paste.

Shichimi togarashi Japanese "seven-flavor chili pepper" spice. Despite its name, it is milder than many Western pepper spices. In addition to hot peppers, the blend includes non-spicy ingredients such as citrus peel and sesame seeds.

Shoyu Japanese word for soy sauce. Locals don't say "soy sauce"—it's always "shoyu."

Sriracha A Thai seasoned hot sauce. Commonly called "rooster sauce" for the label on one of the most prevalent brands.

Sukiyaki no Tomo Japanese "sukiyaki vegetables"; comes in a can and includes mushrooms, yam noodles and bamboo shoots.

Surimi Japanese term for raw fish paste. Used as a base for fish cake, patties or other items (including imitation crab). On the mainland, the term is sometimes used to refer to the cooked product.

Taegu Spicy Korean dried codfish.

Takenoko Japanese term for bamboo shoots. Harvested young, they are boiled before eating. They are not seen much in fresh form, but are readily found canned in Asian grocery stores.

Tako Japanese word for octopus ("heʻe" in Hawaiian).

Takuan Japanese pickled turnip. Can be yellow or white.

Tofu Soybean curd of Chinese origin, popular in Japan and other Asian countries.

Wakame Japanese term for another type of kelp, commonly seen in soups or salads. It is not as thick as konbu and when dried (as usually seen in stores) it often resembles tea leaves, rather than large sheets. It sometimes rehydrates as long strips which may need to be cut smaller for use.

Warabi Japanese term for fiddlehead fern ("hōʻiʻo" in Hawaiian, also known as "pohole").

Wasabi Known as Japanese horseradish but green and hotter.

Yuzu The Japanese word for a type of Asian citrus. The fruits are round, resembling grapefruit, and have a somewhat similar tart flavor. The juice is used in marinades and sauces, anywhere a lemon or lime might be used in Western cooking.

INDEX

About the Author

Arnold Hiura is a writer, editor, curator and media consultant. He and his wife, Eloise, are partners in MBFT Media, which provides a variety of communications and creative services to Hawai'i companies and community organizations. Arnold previously served as editor of *The Hawai'i Herald* and curated the Japanese American National Museum's "Bento to Mixed Plate" exhibit that toured the Hawaiian Islands, Los Angeles, the Smithsonian Institution in Washington, D.C., and museums in Japan.

Arnold's book, *Kau Kau: Cuisine and Culture in the Hawaiian Islands*, won the Hawai'i Book Publishers Association's Ka Palapala Po'okela Award of Excellence in Cookbooks in 2010. He followed that up the subsequent year by co-writing chef Alan Wong's *The Blue Tomato*, which won both the Ka Palapala Po'okela and the prestigious IACP (International Association of Culinary Professionals) Cookbook Award ("Chefs & Restaurants" category winner) in New York. His food writing credits also include Chef Russell Siu's *On the Rise* (1996) and Chef Sam Choy's *Cooking from the Heart* (1995).

In 2012, Arnold and Eloise moved to the sugar plantation town of Pāpa'ikou on the Big Island of Hawai'i, about five miles north of Hilo, where he was born and raised.

SURIMI AND POKE PATTIES

BAKED SAL

SAKE-SOY BRAISED SHORT RIBS

K AND BEANS

KIM CHEE SMC

pan-roasted kampachi

sardines an

'OPIHI TWO WAYS

SPIC'

y Braised Short Ribs

PIPI KAULA POKE

Braised Pork Belly Bau B

CHICKEN HEKKA

RIVER 'OPAE

SPAM MU

iled shrimp

LOCO MOCO

TO

GARLIC SALT-AND-PEPPER SHRIMP

KABOCHA AN

lmon salad

'opihi two ways